The People's Histo

North Shields

Memories of Fish 'n' Ships

by Ron Wright

A sequel to Beyond the Piers

Bell Street, Fish Quay, *circa* 1920.

Previous Page: A bit of fun on the Fish Quay, 2002 – Albert Suniga, proprietor of Riverview Fisheries.

Copyright © Ron Wright 2003

First published in 2003 by

The People's History Ltd
Suite 1, Byron House
Seaham Grange Business Park
Seaham, Co. Durham, SR7 0PY

ISBN 1 902527 40 2

Contents

LT 235 *Silver Seas*. Lowestoft registered drifters were frequent visitors to North Shields, often crewed by local men.

Introduction

There are many ways whereby men earn a living. Some we see everyday as they go about their daily work or business – the window cleaner, the postman, the builder, the lorry driver and so one might go on. There are also others who work out of sight of the public eye – the oilrig workers, the lonely shepherd of the hills and the deep-sea fishermen.

The sea has no conscience and it is a foolish man who does not give the sea respect. The sea treats all men alike – rich, poor, good, bad, wealthy or powerful. They all get the same treatment. Fishing ports have many widows. The fishing industry might be almost finished and destroyed by the faceless bureaucrats of Brussels but there was once a time when for every coal miner killed another four fishermen were lost at sea. The old saying, 'Ask not the price of fish for it is paid for in men's lives' was so true.

North Shields Fish Quay in 1947 when
fish was in abundance.

The town of North Shields owes its beginnings, commercial success and livelihood to the sea and the river but like many towns and cities prosperity and fashion dictated that the centre move away from the river. The regional capital, Newcastle-upon-Tyne, has successfully gentrified the Quayside returning the focus of the city back towards the riverside and this is now being complemented by Gateshead on the south side of the River Tyne.

The riverside of North Shields is about to be redeveloped and hopefully not destroyed like so many other schemes have done in this area. Many of these schemes have been developed and initiated by people from outside of the area who have little knowledge or interest in the cultural heritage of the locality.

This book seeks to complement my first book *Beyond the Piers – A Tribute to the Fishermen of North Shields*. The first book concentrated on life at sea but this volume concentrates more on life ashore together with further accounts of life at sea. It is however firmly anchored around the river, fishing, local characters and eccentrics and the cold grey sea beyond the piers.

My first book was very well received. It is hoped that this additional book will continue to be of interest to maritime historians, local historians and people with a general interest in North Shields, the sea and the fishing industry, its culture and the people who made it what it was.

Perhaps this poem titled *Sad Memories* may put today in context. These thoughts surely echo around all of the once great fishing ports of this country.

> *I walk along the Union Quay to find*
> *These changing years have left me behind*
> *Memories sadly in my mind, that only dreams fulfil*
>
> *The Fish Quay is cold and bare*
> *I dream of the trawlers once tied up there*
> *Of crowds of fishermen who were everywhere, but now it's quiet and still*
>
> *The life I knew has passed and gone*
> *But ghosts forever live on and on.*
> *It seems like yesterday but no, it happened so many years ago.*

RIVERSIDE STREETS TANNERS BANK TO THE FISH QUAY GUT

'And make sure they are fresh my man!' Rich and poor on the Quayside in the early part of the last century.

The town of North Shields can trace its beginnings back to the 13th century but it was not until the 18th century that it developed in the way that we can still see today. From being a small community of salt panners and fishermen, where its fortunes ebbed and flowed like the incessant tide, the arrival of the industrial age, the birth of the railways, the nearness of an abundant and cheap coal supply, and the use of steam to propel fishing, towing, cargo and passengers vessels created today's town of North Shields.

The name North Shields has been in use for many centuries but in the 15th century the local inhabitants continued to refer to the town as the 'Low Lights' as the town commenced and sprawled along the riverside from roughly the current location of the Low Lights lighthouse.

This book seeks to concentrate on the original town along the river where the majority of the working class lived in the narrow, crowded, squalid, tenement streets of Low Street and the surrounding area. All the main businesses and industries associated with the town were housed in this area, confined and restricted to a two-mile stretch of the river.

At the turn of the 19th century the Low Street of North Shields was two rows of Tudor Houses, which ran from the Low Lights to the Bull Ring (opposite the current ferry landing). The greater part of the street was only eleven feet wide but for short distances this widened from between sixteen and twenty-five feet. On the river side of the street, short lanes and quays led to the river's edge where the houses were packed tightly together as they crowded around little courts off the street or extended out on quays resting on piles driven into the bed of the river. The houses on the opposite side of the road jostled against one another up the hillside where steep flights of stairs gave access to the houses behind Low Street and the bank top above.

Along these streets, where William Wouldhave (the inventor of the lifeboat) was born, was a chaotic mix of industry, crime and commercial outlets. Here bakers, brewers, block and mast makers, braziers and tin men, tallow chandlers, grocers, sail makers, rope makers, coopers, spirit merchants, clothes dealers, thieves, swindlers, pick pockets and beggars plied their trade amidst a plethora of public houses – ninety-six in the stretch of one mile.

Many of these public houses had grand sounding names that did not reflect their general state of decay although many of the names used fired the imagination and tickled the fancy. Between the Bull Ring and the Low Lights could be found the establishments of the Steam Packet, Half Moon, Hope Tavern, The Ark, Black Boy, the Fox and Lamb, the Jerusalem Coffee House, The Lighthouse, the Ship and Whale and the Raffled Anchor to name just a few.

These public houses would have a bar for the working classes and a bar parlour, which was a superior room where shipowners, captains, merchants and tradesmen met to discuss business. In and out would pass pedlars, pie men and vendors of food.

The Rising Sun stood on Tyne Street, 100 yards east of the High Lights. This public house plied its trade from about 1830 until it was demolished in 1960. The Old High Light is behind the pub.

Eventually in 1763 the town began to grow upwards away from the banks of the River Tyne as the prosperous shipowners and businessmen built houses above the banks in Dockwray Square where they had a commanding view of the river and the harbour. Toll Square and Tyne Terrace quickly followed for the shipowners and shipbuilders. However, the development would suffer from a lack of water and drainage facilities that would never be solved. The elegant square would eventually deteriorate into slums and be condemned by the late 1950s.

Dockwray Square was named after the Rector of Tynemouth, the Reverend Thomas Dockwray and from this period onwards the town grew rapidly outwards into the flatlands. With the ongoing regeneration of North Shields, Dockwray Square is now back to its former glory but mystery surrounds a gruesome past.

The Old High Light (seen here in 1962) was built in 1727 and replaced by the new High Light in 1810.

At the beginning of the 19th century medical science was moving forward at a rapid pace and the use of dead bodies for research and teaching was a necessary evil. Due to the demand for dead bodies the criminal elements quickly seized upon the opportunity for quick and easy money. It is a harrowing fact of life at this time that a child of tender years could be hanged for stealing a loaf of bread but the body snatchers, who defiled and rifled the graves of recently deceased people, escaped with a short prison sentence. To protect their dead, relatives were forced to stand guard and keep vigil over their deceased until such time as they ceased to be interest to the body snatchers. Church walls were heightened and spiked.

The infamous duo of Burke and Hare reputedly made their mark in North Shields.

Burke, an Irishman, travelled about the country selling wares, buying old clothes, and collecting skins, human hair and anything else

The Old High Light today – a private dwelling.

that he could sell. In the autumn of 1827 he met William Hare, who kept a sort of beggars hotel or lodging-house in Tanners Close, West Port, Edinburgh under the name of Logs Lodging. In this abode of debauchery, vice, and drunkenness, they commenced a murderous trade, which continued for about twelve months. They exploited the incessant need for dead bodies but this trade consigned them to the infamous annals of history.

In December 1827 a lodger died in the lodging house, an elderly man, tall but stout, whose debauched habits accounted for his death. A coffin was procured, guests invited and the lodger was buried with all due solemnity. However there was no body in the coffin but just a sack full of bark. After the funeral the body snatchers proceeded to find a purchaser and carry the body to its final resting place – the dissecting rooms of Dr Knox, where they received seven pounds ten shillings. So much easy money to such people excited their cupidity. Burke and Hare decided that they would now miss out the middleman and murder victims in order to sell their bodies.

Their first known murder victim was an old woman who was stupefied with drink, and put to death. She was readily sold for ten pounds in December 1827. A bargain was struck whereby Burke and Hare were to receive eight pounds for each 'subject' in the summer, and ten pounds in the winter – no questions asked.

Thirteen more people met their untimely end before Burke and Hare were arrested. Before the trial, an offer was made to Hare to give evidence for the prosecution and in return he would receive immunity and allowed his freedom. Faced with the gallows he gladly accepted the proposal. On 24th December 1828, at the High Court of Judiciary, Edinburgh, the evidence of Hare condemned Burke to the gallows.

But what of Hare, who it was said, was the worst and who first led Burke on, and then gained his freedom by turning King's Evidence. Under the name of Mr Black (not an inappropriate name for him), he was escorted from his cell in the Calton Jail late on a Thursday night. On this cold, sleety night in the month of February he boarded the mail-coach for Dumfries, to get into England where he disappeared and was never heard of again.

The High Lights lighthouse in the days of the disappearance of John Margetts. The High Lights lighthouse stood at the entrance to Dockwray Square, which has been recently rebuilt with new houses.

By now you may be wondering what all this has to do with Dockwray Square and North Shields. In 1826 John Margetts was a paid assistant of Doctor Greenhow who practised medicine in North Shields. At five o'clock in the morning John was sent to deliver medicine to Mrs Gaunt in Tyne Street beside Dockwray Square and was never heard of again. Mr Profit, a mason, heard a scuffle in Tyne Street and heard someone cry out, 'What are you doing to me.' Three men were seen in Tyne Street, and two of the men were leading the other man. They were then seen in Howard Street and Union Street but witnesses assumed that the third man was drunk. Shortly afterwards according to another witness two men were seen dragging a third man along Low Street by the New Quay, the third man crying out that he was being murdered. A broken leatherneck collar was found in the vicinity.

Naters Stairs could have been easily used by the abductors of the unfortunate John Margetts. The stairs lead down from Dockwray Square to the Fish Quay.

Shortly after the disappearance of Margetts, a stallholder by the name of Johnny Aird disappeared without reason from the New Quay where he had been peddling his wares. Upon the arrest of Burke and Hare a local doctor, Doctor Greenhow, asked Mr Park, who had a painter's shop near to Aird's stall, to go to Edinburgh to see if Aird and

Hare were the same man. Why it was believed that there was a connection between Burke and Hare and Aird remains a mystery but the good doctor must have had a strong belief that there was. Aird returned to North Shields making the damning identification 'I have not the slightest doubt that Aird (or Hare) had made away with Margetts and sold his body at Edinburgh.'

And so the story appears to end until sixty years later when the grandson of Mr Parks revealed that no identification had been made of Hare because he had been released and disappeared two days before the arrival of his grandfather. What is the truth, no one will ever know? It may be that Mr Parks never made his damning accusation or that the account by his grandson is hearsay and cannot be validated. However the story, if that is what it may be and not the truth, gives a glimpse of a world far removed from our own but which also has some parallels with our society for we can still be no less violent.

If the inhabitants of North Shields two hundred years ago could accompany us today along the riverside they would see changes, which they would have difficulty in comprehending, but notwithstanding the enormous changes in technology they would still be able to recognise portions of the principle streets along the riverside. Whilst the long narrow streets running parallel with the river have almost disappeared much still remains and which attests to the way of life over the past two centuries.

Bird Street, off Brewery Bank, long since demolished, stood above the Fish Quay close to the start of our walk. The chimney in the centre of the picture belonged to Tyne Brand.

Let us now take a present day walk from east to west through the riverside streets of old North Shields whilst they are still there to detail and remember the rich tapestry of life. The walk will be broken into the streets as they became defined in 1828. Period photographs will be used by way of illustration together with photographs taken in 2002. There is much to see and it will take us some time so in order to allow for a little rest and light refreshment the walk will be broken periodically with a story or two.

Standing at the foot of Tanners Bank or Union Road stands a white building, which is Caley's Ships Chandlers. This building occupies the site of an old flourmill and behind the premises was an old hostelry, the 'Ship in Launch', now long consigned to the history books. To the rear of Caley's the mouth of the River Tyne and the monument to Admiral Lord Collingwood can be clearly discerned.

Caley's Ships Chandlers as it looks today.

The granite piers protecting the mouth of the River Tyne represent to me the encirclement of a mother's arms around her baby. However in the middle years of the 19th century it was so very different. The River Tyne was alive with shipping and commerce yet the river itself was suffering from years of neglect. The commercial centre of Newcastle-upon-Tyne was only interested in trade and maximising their profits. The heavily polluted river was difficult to navigate, as the river was sluggish and wreck and rock strewn. No dredging had taken place and the sailing ships were at the mercy of Mother Nature.

The Shields bar was a constantly shifting shingle, rock and sand bank, which formed across the mouth of the river. Eight hundred feet long and six hundred feet wide, safe negotiation of the bar depended on the tides, the prevailing wind conditions and the depth of the water beneath a ship's keel. At low water there was never more than six feet of water on the bar. In August 1824 there was one of the lowest spring tides that could be remembered. Three Tyne pilots set off to walk across the mouth of Tyne at Tynemouth bar. At high water on that day the bar afforded twenty-four feet and eight inches of clearance, more than sufficient for any vessel of that time but when the pedestrians crossed at low tide there was just two feet of water.

There are nights, in winter, when the booming of the sea rolls inland like the drowned tolling of a funeral bell. The raw-edged shrieking of the wind joins in the tumult. It is easy to imagine a frail ship beating her way through the foam, her captain's eyes wide with fear and apprehension.

No count has ever really been made of the total number of lives lost along these few miles of shore but the number of wrecks stretch into the hundreds over the past two centuries.

In the 19th century a lone body washed up by the tide was not unusual and hardly newsworthy, the assumption being that a vessel had gone down, perhaps as close as just a few miles off the Tyne. In other instances, the firing of a gun from the river's guard ship would warn the townsfolk that a disaster was at that moment happening.

There were many curious and concerned onlookers when on one stormy day in January 1910 the Norwegian barque *Alphonse* ran aground on the Herd Sands, South Shields during a gale. She beached just north of Trow Rocks, spilling part of the cargo she had been carrying. On this occasion no lives were lost amongst her 29-strong crew.

The *Alphonse* aground on the Herd Sands, South Shields.

Often ships were sold for salvage where they lay, together with whatever cargo had survived the inrush of both the sea and looters, who would carry off anything, remotely movable. In one incident the booty from a Russian tallow ship kept the town of South Shields lit for many months.

Many a prayer must have been whispered beneath a mariner's breath as he braved the bar. Given a stiff easterly wind the bar could become a raging maelstrom of sea, spray and foam. Many vessels foundered as they tried to enter or leave the Tyne. It was dangerous to enter and difficult to leave.

Yet despite these problems in the mid 19th century over 1,500 ships were registered from the Port of Tyne (which included Newcastle, North and South Shields) and sailing ships from America, Holland, Greece, France and the Baltic States were frequent visitors.

The majority of these ships were two and three masted barques, brigs, snows and schooners that rarely exceeded 400 registered tons. Although most of these were colliers who plied their trade between Newcastle and London many of them tramped around the world wherever their cargoes and trade took them.

Movement in and out of the Tyne was entirely dependent upon the weather. Prolonged easterly winds prevented vessels from leaving the Tyne. In the winter of 1847/48, at the turn of the year, 1,700 vessels lay wind bound in the Tyne for several weeks. Ten years later 727 vessels were forcibly tied up in the Tyne between North Shields and Jarrow Slake whilst many more lay elsewhere in the river. The number of ships is reputed to have numbered in excess of one thousand and the river must have looked like a forest of masts.

Entering the Tyne in bad weather, or when heavy seas were running, the sailing ships made for an exciting spectacle and in such conditions many thousand of onlookers would gather on the shore. Disaster was never very far away.

On 5th January 1841, in atrocious conditions, the sloop *Newcastle and Berwick Packet* was seen running the bar for the safety of the river. The vessel disappeared in a fury of white foam as she crossed the bar but emerged unscathed, the only ship to enter the river that day. Others were less fortunate.

During the December of 1870 the North East coast suffered from a prolonged period of bad weather. The steamship *Eagle* of London made a run for the river but a heavy sea swamped her and extinguished the fires in her boiler rooms. Another wave almost sent her to the bottom before she drove and stranded on the Herd Sands at South Shields. Shortly after this the 539 ton barque *City of Bristol* failed to make the Tyne entrance and was driven ashore on Tynemouth Long Sands. Within a short period of time the Norwegian Schooner *Amalie* from Stavanger came crashing ashore within sight of the *City of Bristol*.

Later that afternoon the 85 ton Boston schooner *Samuel Bernard* almost made it into the refuge of the harbour when a fierce sea hit her amidships and rolled her over. She disappeared from view and was never seen again. Her crew of seven perished. The crew were made up of the ship's master Captain John Frash, his wife and five children. The vessel sank within 100 yards of the South Pier.

Leaving the harbour for the open seas was slightly less dangerous but nevertheless many vessels succumbed to disaster. Grounding the keel heavily as the vessel 'bounced' over the bar could cause severe leaks that frequently sank a vessel days later whilst on the open seas.

Between 1830 and 1900, one mariner in five lost his life at sea. No other form of occupation had such an attrition rate including deep coal mining. In the same period seventy percent of all Tyne sailing ships were lost at sea as they foundered, caught fire, ran ashore and became wrecked, were run down by other vessels or just disappeared and were recorded as 'lost at sea'.

The coastal and continental trade in coal made up the vast amount of trade for the Tyne sailing ships. In 1836 11,226 ships cleared the Tyne loaded with coal for all over the world whilst a further 148 carried other goods. In the following year it was recorded that 3,845 ships carried coal from the Tyne to London alone.

Two of the last sailing ships which were regular visitors to the North East in the 1930s, in particular Blyth and Seaham, were the *Hilda* and the *Waterwitch*. Neither of these vessels were by now locally owned and both were in foreign ownership. However, they represented the type of vessel that made up the vast fleets of Tyne owned vessels.

The *Hilda* was lost off Hartlepool in 1930 when she was run down by a steam trawler and sliced in two. Fully laden with coal just shipped from Blyth, she went to the bottom within two minutes. The *Waterwitch*, which was built in 1871, ended her days training pilots for Gravesend and the Thames.

The *207* ton barquentine *Waterwitch* being escorted into the Tyne by the pilot boat *Queen of the May* in the 1920s.

The North and South Piers did not protect the mouth of the River Tyne until 1894 having taken almost half a century to complete at a cost of £1,500,000. Work on the North Pier commenced in October 1855 and on the South Pier in March 1856. However the fury of the North Sea quickly exposed a weakness in the North Pier.

On 2nd and 3rd December 1867, following an extended period of stormy weather, 240 feet of the north face of the North Pier and 250 feet of the north face of the South Pier fell into the sea and was washed away. Once again the foundations had been found to be inadequate and 36 ton foundation blocks were utilised to affect the repairs.

After a prolonged period of storms between 22nd and 23rd January 1897 the pier was breached. A year later another great storm made a clean breach in the pier and carried away a few hundred feet completely cutting off the lighthouse. This required a new section of pier to be built to a different design and with deeper foundations. This was not the first time that the pier had been breached.

The North Pier breached in 1897.

Another view of the breached North Pier. The lighthouse keepers had a perilous journey to work in the bad weather and in the dark.

The North Pier in 1912. Two ferries regularly ran from the Pier, one across to South Shields and the larger ferry up the river to Newcastle.

Closer towards the Fish Quay the familiar site of the statue of Admiral Lord Collingwood overlooks the River Tyne from his commanding position on the headland. The monument was erected in 1845 and four of the thirty-two pound guns from his ship, the *Royal Sovereign*, stand guard at the base of the monument. Cuthbert Collingwood was a member of an old Northumberland family, and was the son of Cuthbert Collingwood, a merchant, of Newcastle-upon-Tyne, and Milcha, daughter of Reginald Dobson of Barwess, Westmorland. Born in 1750 at Newcastle, Cuthbert was educated at the Newcastle Grammar School and when he first went to sea as a boy only thirteen years old, he was reputedly better educated than many of the officers who had been to university. Collingwood's first command was the *Hinchinbrooke*, to which he was appointed in 1780, when at the time his good friend, Horatio Nelson was promoted to another ship in the West Indies.

Collingwood fought in nearly all of the big naval actions in the wars with France and Spain, including Bunker Hill (1775), the Glorious First of June (1794), Cape St Vincent (1797) and Trafalgar (1805).

The Campaign of Trafalgar 1803-05, one of the most famous and strategically significant victories of the age of the sail, was not an isolated event, but rather a culmination of a campaign that began as soon as war was resumed in May 1803, the ultimate aim being the invasion of Great Britain by Napoleon and his allied forces. In his ship the *Royal Sovereign*, Collingwood led the fleet to victory at the Battle of Trafalgar following the death of Nelson. As a reward he received a peerage, and adopted the title of Baron Collingwood of Caldburne and

Hethpoole in Northumberland, with a pension of £2,000 per year awarded by Parliament. After Trafalgar he was also appointed Commander-in-Chief in the Mediterranean, and continued to serve in this capacity, but his life's race was nearly run. His health had long been failing, though he does not appear to have realised the very serious nature of his illness until too late. He died on the 7th March 1810 at his post in obedience to the call of duty. His body was brought to England, and, after lying in state in the Painted Hall in Greenwich, was buried in the crypt of St Paul's by the side of Nelson.

Lord Collingwood was a typical north countryman, never unduly elated at success or depressed by failure, caring little for popular applause, quiet and retiring in his ways, anxious only to serve his country to the best of his ability.

Lord Collingwood's monument stands guard at the mouth of the Tyne.

Turning westward we can now meander along Union Road towards the Fish Quay with the new fish processing outlets on our left-hand side. This fairly recent development occupies the site of the old hostelries of the Half Moon Inn and Waggs Inn. Some of the old smoke houses, where millions of kippers were produced, can be seen behind the new buildings and the New Dolphin public house.

The famous Tyne Brand factory would have been on our right-hand side but it was demolished in August 2002. The Tyne Brand name was famous throughout the world for its tinned herring in tomato sauce and a history of the factory is detailed in my book *Beyond the Piers* titled 'An entrepreneur, silver fish and tin cans.'

Crossing the street known as Brewhouse Bank, the tiny Low Lights Tavern reminds us of the public houses of yesteryear as it nestles at the foot of the bank almost unnoticed by passers-by, unless of course you are after a drink.

The Low Lights Tavern has been serving beer to thirsty sailors and fishermen for over four hundred years.

We have now reached one of the least imposing buildings on the Fish Quay on Union Road and one that is a sad state of neglect. Fortunately the building has been saved from demolition and is to be preserved for the future. The building to which I refer is the office of Richard Irvin and Sons Ltd. There is little doubt that the contribution of Richard Irvin to the growth of North Shields was inextricably linked and a separate section follows this first part of the walk to pay tribute to this man and some of his associates.

The New Dolphin Public House, formerly the Staithes Inn, stands opposite the offices of Richard Irvin and Sons. The circular object at the door is a whale jawbone which was caught in the nets of the *Star Of Peace* in 1998 twenty miles off the coast. The *Star of Peace* (*below*) was scrapped as part of the decommissioning programme.

Looking towards the river from Irvin's office much of what remains of the old part of North Shields becomes evident. In 1672 during the reign of Charles II the country was at war with the Netherlands and it was considered expedient to build a fort to protect the entrance to the River Tyne. The fort was named after Lord Thomas Clifford and lasted as a fort until May of 1926 when the Tyne Electrical Engineers transferred to the Territorial Army Centre in Tynemouth. The fort stood on the site of a previous fort (little is known of this earlier fort), and was surrounded by stonewalls. Clifford's Fort dominated the entrance to the river, with small turrets built into the walls at every turn; the whole site was surrounded by a moat and manned by the North Shields and Tynemouth Volunteers. In its day the fort was a formidable defence system with its thirty-one pound guns sticking out through the battlements but nowadays the fort is more benign as office accommodation. The fort was never really put to the test for the purpose that it was built but it did succumb to damage from the sea. Three times in the early part of the 19th century parts of the walls were washed away by storms and on each occasion the walls were repaired.

Close to the fort there stands a building where no building should be. This is the railway station for the Fish Quay, which now houses a taxi firm. Now I know you may think that my research has gone awry here because there has never been a railway passenger line down to the Fish Quay and you would be correct in that statement. However this did not stop the town council in building a railway station at this location in an effort to coerce the North Eastern Railway Company to build a line. After the railway station was built the railway company stood by their decision that such a line was not financially viable.

'The train now arriving at the Fish Quay is … ' No train ever arrived here! This taxi office was built by the local council as a railway station where no trains ran and no railway line was laid.

Within the walls that protected Clifford's Fort but forming no part of the defence system stood the Low Light lighthouse. This lighthouse and its newer sister, the High Lights lighthouse, were two of the most prominent landmarks in the area from land, sea or river and they continue to dominate the skyline. The first Low Lights lighthouse was built in 1727 but the High Lights lighthouse followed shortly after that at the foot of Beacon Street.

By the beginning of the 19th century the lighthouses were no longer positioned correctly due to the changes in the river and on 2nd March 1805 at a meeting of local shipowners in North Shields it was resolved to obtain an Act of Parliament for the building of two new lighthouses, the cost to be defrayed by charging all arriving vessels 1 penny per ton of each ship. On 29th September 1807 the foundation stones for the new High and Low Lights was laid and both lighthouses were built in less than three years. Both lights were lit for the first time on 1st May 1810. These were not the first lighthouses built in this area, the first recorded lighthouse dating back to 1539.

The Low Lights looking across towards the High Lights. Safe entry into the river was guaranteed when both lighthouses were lined up in a straight line.

The lights burned brightly in both lighthouses for over a hundred years until they were decommissioned. The High Lights lighthouse is now a private dwelling house that in October 2002 went on sale for the asking price of £415,000. The Low Lights lighthouse is currently under restoration.

Before we finish this short walk let us go beyond the Low Lights and around to the small bay known as the Fish Quay sands. A scarred and almost derelict jetty juts out into the river for no apparent reason. It seems to have no use now but until 1969 a little yellow hut that was Lloyds Hailing Station stood at the end of the jetty. Nearby was the Lifeboat house, now demolished, which used to launch the lifeboat down a ramp with a spectacular splash of dirty grey river foam.

The Fish Quay Sands with Lloyds Hailing Station at the end of the jetty. In the herring season the herring were gutted on the Quay, salted and sealed in wooden casks.

The hailing station provided by Lloyds Shipping Agency recorded traffic movements into and out of the Port to satisfy legal requirements and to wire out destinations and safe arrivals to those with an interest, such as owners, agents and the relatives of those at sea.

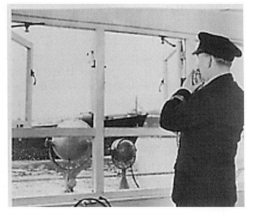

As a ship left the Tyne a voice would boom out on the tannoy from the hailing station, 'What's your name, where you bound.' One old wag recounts the following conversation with a Dutch coaster. I make no claim that this conversation ever took place.

Hailing Station:	'What's yer name?'
Reply:	'Annar.'
Hailing Station:	'What's yer name?'
Reply:	'Annar.'
Hailing Station:	'Ah kna ye kna, but ah need t' kna.'
Reply:	'Annar.'

Lloyds Hailing Station, the last one of its kind in the country.

Lloyds Hailing Station closed at midnight on 30th September 1969 after recording the movements of Tyne shipping for more than half a century. For Bill Davidson, the last keeper of the registers, this ended a happy thirteen years of work and retirement became a reality.

But it had not all been plain sailing for the keepers of Lloyds registers in their warm snug hut. Sid Lyons was on duty in the station in March 1960 when the Norwegian Oil Tanker *Hoegh Spear* came into the river. Sid never had time to ask the master for the identity of the ship and their destination on the river. The large tanker sheered off course and headed straight for the hailing station and Sid in it. Sid used to commute back and forwards to work on a little moped, which was started by pedalling furiously and then dropping a lever to start the engine. It is reputed that Sid pedalled that fast that he qualified for the Olympic trials as he struggled to start the engine and disappeared down the jetty in a pall of blue two stroke fumes as the oil tanker crashed through the jetty demolishing the hailing station in its wake.

The Fish Quay Sands and jetty were a hive of industry during the herring season. The local labour force was supplemented by the Scots fishing girls during the season and the following personal account came from the members and staff of the Stockdale/Elms Day Centre.

Memories of the Scottish Fishing Girls

The old joke, that the only good thing to come out of Scotland is the A1, is not one Florrie Higgins would agree with.

For years, Florrie worked as a filleter in the smoke houses that abounded on North Shields Fish Quay, and many of the scores of friends she made were Scottish girls who followed the filleting work around the country.

Scots fishing girls at work on the Quay.

'A lot of the girls from the North East, Scotland and East Anglia followed the herring shoals to Shields, Yarmouth and the Scottish ports,' she explained. 'They would get digs, work all hours of the day, and when the herring moved on, so would they.' She added, 'I can't believe it's a job that today's youngsters would be over keen on. Even the highly skilled girls could be easily spotted by the cuts on their hands. Your fingers got so numb you could cut yourself to the bone and not feel it, but we all loved the Quay. After following the herring it was like coming home for a lot of them, even though the work was hard.'

Florrie maintained her links with the Quayside until she was well into her 70s. Many a fisherman will probably still remember her welcome cups of tea and friendly chat at the Seamen's Mission, where she worked in later years till her long-overdue retirement.

One recipe that she still remembers was given to her by a Scottish girl. 'We became friends and she made it one day for us at my mother's home. It's still a family favourite.'

'Part-boil about 1lb of potatoes and 4oz chopped onion in a

North Shields Fish Quay when the herring drifters were packed in like sardines in a can.

Three North Shields lasses – Hilda Telford, Irene Tweddle, but the third woman is unknown.

pint of water, add about 12ozs of smoked cod or haddock and half a pint of milk, and bring back to boil and taste for seasoning. Simmer gently for 15 minutes. Mash the fish, onions and potatoes together, return to the stock and serve with crusty bread.'

No memories of earlier days in North Shields are more detailed or vivid than the herring season and the bustle and excitement it brought to the Fish Quay. Florrie Higgins recalls it as, 'like the circus coming to town, all the extra people, extra work; everything hustle and bustle.'

Jean Jolly remembers the catches being unloaded. 'Mountains of shining silver coming off the boats, like someone emptying a bank. And I suppose for North Shields it was like that, bringing money to the town.'

Elizabeth Bell, more practically was aware of 'a little bit more prosperity, a bit more cash around in the town. A good season brought smiles to most faces.' For mother, counting the farthings and halfpennies, it meant a welcome source of cheap nutritious food for the family. Betty Waugh's cart was a familiar sight then, carrying the herring to fish shops around the town. 'Fresh herring, four a penny!' was a welcome sound to many hard-pressed homes with young mouths to feed.

The above is an extract from a handout prepared many years ago by the members of the Stockdale/Elms Day centre. This centre is now no more and it is believed that those remembering these happy times have departed from this mortal earth.

Tynemouth Lifeboat *Tynesider* being launched from beside Lloyds Hailing Station.

RICHARD IRVIN, OTHER NORTH SHIELDS ENTREPRENEURS AND MEMORIES OF FISHING

Richard Irvin, a man of vision and a native of North Shields.

Richard Irvin was the founder of one of the most successful group of Victorian companies in this area and must have been an outstanding personality. He possessed those rare gifts of business acumen, vision and not least, self-belief and determination. His business empire was to stretch across the world. However although he was the most successful of the North Shields families he was not alone in exploiting the riches of the cold seas where the most fish can be found.

Richard Irvin was born of humble origins in North Shields in 1852 and by the time he was 16 years old he was a marine store dealer and later fish salesman. Three years later he was the part owner of a sailing trawler called the *Zenith*. At this time the use of steam to power fishing vessels was unknown and supplies of fish were dependent on small sailing craft from fishing villages on the east coast of England and Scotland. Fish catches were entirely dependent upon the prevailing weather conditions.

Significantly the first steam trawling venture in Britain was created in North Shields when William Purdy converted the paddle tug *Messenger* into a trawler in 1877 and within two trips had proved to all his doubters that the application of steam for fishing was not only viable but necessary. Large quantities of fish had been caught in calm weather when the sailing trawlers and drifters would have been useless. Irvin recognised the benefits and was soon the owner of his first steam trawler the *Enterprise*.

Fish Quay, *circa* 1900.

Irvin, never short of enterprise realised that Aberdeen was destined to become a leading fishing port. He sent his son John Irvin to Aberdeen and opened his first branch office there in 1890. His business capabilities were such that they complemented his father's drive and soon the Aberdeen office was highly successful. This marked the start of many such ventures. Branch offices and agents of the company were established in the ports of Aberdeen, Great Yarmouth, Lowestoft, Peterhead, Blyth, Lerwick, Stornaway, Castlebay, Mallaig, Downings Bay, Milford Haven as well as North Shields.

For three decades tugs and trawlers would continue to use paddles, even though the much more efficient propeller had been developed in the 1830s. However, the propeller triumphed and Irvin along with S.F. Purdy and Co, R. Hastie and Sons, W.H. Storey and Eustace Smith created substantial fishing fleets, many of which were based at North Shields. This led to North Shields becoming a substantial fishing port for the first part of the 20th century.

George Purdy, trawler owner outside of Christ Church, Tynemouth.

This was the heyday of herring fishing with over 300 boats fishing from the port in the season and 110 steam trawlers in the winter months of 1897. Richard Irvin was the founder of the East Coast Steam Drifters Ltd, a company based in Great Yarmouth to exploit the herring fishing industry. The growth in fish landed at North Shields grew in excess of 2000% in the space of 20 years when the landings of fish increased from 406 tons in 1877 to 8,569 tons in 1897.

In 1901 Irvin built and opened the Shields Ice and Cold Storage Company to supplement the ice making facilities on the Fish Quay. Always eager to expand his business interests Irvin recognised that there was an over abundance of fish being landed which was outstripping demand. Large quantities of prime haddock were being sold to the local guano factory. Seizing upon the opportunity he expanded the facilities of the Shields Ice and Cold Storage Company to create a cannery and started to can haddock and then herring. Canned haddock was not popular so he swiftly switched to herring, which was being caught in copious amounts, and he never looked back.

Shields Engineering and Dry Dock, colloquially known as the 'Haddock Shop', followed in collaboration with other trawler owners to repair and build the steam trawlers and drifters that formed the mainstay of their business. The original dry dock can still be seen by the edge of the Dolphin Quays housing complex, which now occupies the site. A separate section on the Haddock Shop and the personal experiences of Mike Ennis can be found in a later chapter. Trawlers were registered as belonging to this company.

By 1913, only 40 years after he purchased his first sailing trawler Irvin was head of a huge business, the largest of its kind in the world.

Shields Engineering and Dry Dock, which became known locally as the 'Haddock Shop'.

Local girls waiting for the herring drifters to land their catch. From right to left: Nellie Wadey, Irene Tweddle, Lizzie Snowdon. Ena Cullen, unknown, Ina Bell. Mary Craig is sitting on the barrel facing the camera. Hilda Telford is far left.

Right: Fish on their way to the auctioneer who was frequently Richard Irvin himself.

Below: An auction underway of the day's catch. The smoke stack of a Yarmouth drifter can be seen in the background.

This Victorian entrepreneur remained firmly rooted in North Shields where despite his varied and pressing business interests he spent a great deal of his time in public life and dealing with public affairs. He joined the Town Council in 1890 and was Mayor of Tynemouth in 1897 and 1898. In 1903 he was elected an Alderman and a year later he became a Justice of the Peace. Richard Irvine retired from business in 1920 and died within a year of his retirement.

Many North Shields trawlers ended up in the warm waters off the South African coast but many went searching for whales in the hostile South Atlantic. His fleet even included a four masted schooner, which was fitted with a steam engine.

A Sunday service on the Quayside for the fishing fleet.

The *Isle of Jura* was owned by Irvin's and was used in their whaling enterprise in the Falkland Islands in the 1930s.

Richard Irvine's empire is no more, a casualty of the massive decline in the home fishing industry. However his South African business still thrives. The company's history goes back to 1910, when George Irvin (a son of Richard Irvin) and Charles Johnson began a fishing company operating out of Cape Town harbour. The two partners pioneered the trawling industry in South Africa and today I&J is the country's leading fishing company.

Irvin & Johnson (I&J) is the largest supplier of fresh fish to the South African market. The company operates one of the largest trawling fleets in the Southern Hemisphere, fishing in an area of some 122,400 square miles of the Indian and Atlantic oceans. The company's fleet of 42 vessels includes factory/freezer, wet fish and crustacean trawlers based in Cape Town, Walvis Bay, Mossel Bay, Port Elizabeth and Durban harbours.

The fishing fleet trawls mainly for hake in South African and Namibian waters and also fishes for mackerel, horse mackerel, pilchards, monkfish, kingklip and various species of local fish.

The modern day South African trawler, *George Irvin*.

The Wet Fish Fleet consists of thirteen vessels, most of which are of very modern design. These vessels do not spend more than nine days at sea, after which the catch is discharged immediately on landing and the vessel returns to sea.

There are ten vessels in the Factory Freezer Fleet, three of which are Distant Water Vessels primarily catching horse mackerel. The larger the vessels are, the greater the freezing capacity, thus enabling the vessel to utilise its capabilities better and stay at sea for longer periods between 25 days and 40 days. The freezer holds can store between 350 tons and 800 tons of fish depending on the size of the vessel.

The Cape Town trawling operation has one of the largest marine engineering facilities in the southern hemisphere. The South African industry one century later is replicating the North Shields experience.

Another Successful Venture

At the turn of the last century the Yarmouth River must have presented an impressive appearance. During the late autumn months and at the height of the herring season the harbour mouth and river was alive with paddle tugs busily fussing around the innumerable sailing luggers of the local fleet, together with the visiting Scottish luggers, with just a sprinkling of the new age steam herring drifters. It was a time of great change in the herring industry, brought about mainly by the introduction of steam propulsion and it was a North Shields man who was to be instrumental in assisting the already premier herring port in the country.

The introduction of steam propelling machinery to fishing vessels at Yarmouth had its embryonic beginnings in the early 1870s, but it was to be some considerable time before owners overcame their prejudice of steam vessels. Like many great inventions and innovations there is always reluctance to embrace technology. Sceptics announced that it would never work, as the noise of a thrashing propeller would scare the fish away. This theory completely ignored the fact that whilst the vessel was fishing for herring and lying to her nets, her steam machinery would be inactive.

Two hundred and twenty miles north of Great Yarmouth lay the River Tyne, which was once one of the greatest areas of shipbuilding. In August 1899 the well-known shipbuilding and repair yards of Smith's Dock, North Shields was managed by Eustace Smith, who had assumed control of the family business in 1882. He had quickly amalgamated it with the already well-established business of H.S. Edwards & Sons, and the shipbuilding firm of Edwards Brothers, situated at the old Hepples Shipyard and Slipway. This last named company specialised in building the new age steam trawlers and other types of small vessels.

Following the take-over, it was discovered that four steel hulled steam herring drifters were on the building stocks. These four boats were a new departure for the Edwards Company, who, perhaps with an eye to the future, could see a big demand for steam powered steel hulled fishing vessels of smaller proportions to the already well-established larger steam trawlers.

These four vessels were completed by Smith's Dock over the following ten months, and in the meantime efforts were made at Yarmouth to try and dispose of them to some forward thinking fishing boat owner, or owners. However the local fishermen were biased against steel hulled vessels arguing that the salt used in the herring trade would corrode the steel hulls and Smith's Dock representative at Yarmouth failed in his efforts to get a bid for them.

Smith's Dock knew from their own experience as ship repairers that this was a mistaken idea, as they frequently had through their hands steel vessels, whose freight was salt, and that this type of cargo did no material damage to the hull.

As the herring fishing at Yarmouth appeared a profitable business, and finding that they could not sell the new vessels, Smith's Dock determined that it would be profitable for them to work the boats themselves with local skippers and crew. Early in June 1900, the first of these four new boats arrived in Great Yarmouth. The vessel created quite a stir along the fish wharf, as at that time, only eleven steam drifters had been registered at Yarmouth.

Yarmouth drifter *Seven* owned by Smith's Docks. Here she is on trials before being registered as YH 542.

On 7th June, the grey-hulled new arrival from the Tyne was registered at the port as a fishing vessel, with the unromantic name of *One* bestowed on her, and with the Fishing Number YH 463. This was the pattern set for all the other drifters that were to come into the new fleet, all to receive a numerical name, and which was to develop into one of the largest steam herring drifter fleets in the country.

The first four boats to arrive at Yarmouth during that summer were initially registered in the name of Eustace Smith, who held the controlling interest in the new company until his untimely death in 1902. The registered ownership was changed to that of Smith's Dock Trust Company on the 20th September 1900, the same day that saw Richard Sutton, a very well known and experienced Yarmouth fishing vessel owner, become the first manager of the newly formed company.

During *One's* initial autumn herring season at Yarmouth in 1900, she earned over £3000 for her owners, not a bad beginning. A total of four hundred and four Scottish fishing vessels worked out of the port that autumn, a figure that included seventy steam powered boats.

The Trust Company's first drifter *One*, continued to give good service to her owners and within the next two years a further thirty-four drifters were registered following the numeric principle. The Smith's Dock fleet became the largest single fleet using Great Yarmouth as their homeport.

The Great War signalled the demise and end of the red funnelled fleet in Great Yarmouth as the abstraction level for naval duties and pressing matters back on Tyneside ran down the fleet. However these sturdy little and effective sea boats continued on for many many years. The last of the fleet YH 874 *Three*, which was built in 1908, was scrapped in 1957. So much for the prophecy that the salt from the herring would corrode her steel hull!

A full catalogue of trawlers and drifters which were registered at North Shields and which carried the port registration SN are detailed in my book *Beyond the Piers* but it was always accepted that this list did not fully document the steam trawlers and drifters which used North Shields as their home port but which carried other port registrations. The task of documenting a more complete listing was daunting and enormous but in order to redress the balance and try and supplement my initial research I have now been able to determine the details of trawlers and drifters owned or managed by North Shields based individuals or companies.

A summary of the numbers of trawlers/drifters/whalers owned by the various major contributors to the prosperity of North Shields is as follows:

Owner	Number of Ships	
Richard Irvine and Sons Ltd	197	Trawlers and Drifters
Irvin and Johnston, South Africa	106	Trawlers and Whalers
Smith's Dock Drifters	45	Drifters
Prince Line (W.H. Storey)	43	Trawlers and Drifters
S.F. Purdy and Co and family	24	Trawlers and Drifters
Robert Hastie and Sons and family	23	Trawlers and Drifters
Kergulin Sealing and Whaling (Irvin)	18	Trawlers and Whalers
Shields Engineering (Irvin and others)	9	Trawlers

The majority of trawlers and drifters based at North Shields tended to be registered from the port and carried the SN designation before their number. However this was not mandatory and some trawlers fished for long periods from North Shields with local crews whilst registered elsewhere.

The following trawlers and drifters were not SN registered but were regularly seen in the port. This is not a complete listing but is derived from people's memories and boats owned by local families. Unfortunately the Quaymaster's notes and the records from the Lloyds Hailing Station cannot be traced.

Name of Vessel	Port Registration	Year Built
Abergeldie	A 391	1915
Agnes Purdy	A 138	1919
Anchor of Hope	PD 484	1903
Arlette	GY 1315	1918
Aro	A 333	Not known
Arthur H Johnson	YH 402	1913
Avondale	H 166	1918
Belldock	GY 367 / SN 11	1917
Belton	LT 301	1918
Ben Hope	LT 352	1900
Ben Ardna	A 417	1917

A 40 *Ben Chourn*.

Ben Arthur	A 762	Not known
Ben Breac	A 705	1916
Ben Chourn	A 40	1914
Ben Gulvain	A 751	1965
Ben Heilem	A 118	1914
Ben Heilem	A 553	1961
Ben Idris	GN 7	1931
Ben Loyal	A 256	1961
Ben Lui	A 166	1971
Ben Lui	A 715	1953
Ben Meidie	A 319	1959
Ben Screel	A 105	1953
Ben Urie	A 739	1916
Braconmoor	A 164	Not known
City of London	YH 57	1897
County of Fife	KY 572	1896
Cygnet	SH 103	1883
D W Fitzgerald	A 629	1916
Dorileen	A 412	1917
Earl of Buchan	PD 242	1916
Elcho	GN 68	1908
Emblem	LT 785	1907
F & G G	YH 87	1914
Fort William	GY 712	1903
Georgette	A 352	1919
General Gordon	WK 268	Not known

The fine lines of A 715 *Ben Lui*.

A 105 *Ben Screel*.

PD 242 *Earl of Buchan*.

Grace	LH 1095	1882
Griffin	GY 1240	1903
Henriette	GY 1326 / A 205	1918
Inchgower	A 265	1919
Integrity	KY 173	1907
Jean Edmonds	A 174	1916
Judith Purdy	A 220	1919
Kincorth	A263	1909
Kitty	SD 276	1897
Leam	GY 367 / SN 11	1917
Linnet	GY 388	1891
Lolist	LT 427 / BCK 29	1914
Lottie	YH 434	1899
Lowestoft	YH 416	1900
Lune	GY 1143	1900
Lydia Long	YH 567	1917
Lynne Purdy	A 60	1917
Marie Roze	PD 372	Not known
Mary Anne Purdy	GN 70	1918
Maryland	LT 506	1902
Masterpiece	YH 407	1907
Mon Ami	YH 178	1901
Ocean Fisher	A 233	1919
Osprey	SH 79	1892
Peep O'Day	LT 461	1898
Petrel	M 151	1885

Lolist whilst carrying the Buckie registration BCK 29.

Peterborough	HL 41	1897
Placeo	LT 533	1910
Prolific	LT 418	1906
Ribble	GY 1159	1900
Roulette	LT 1041	1907
River Garry	A 233	1919
River Leven	GY 293	1918
Sabina	A 362	1909
Southward Ho	A 16	1919
Sunray	A 669	1891
Sunrise	A 648	1891
The Prince	YH 878	1904
The Queen	YH 879	1904
The Throne	YH 234	1913
Tumby	DE 10	1918
Ugiebank	PD 85	1914
Upton Castle	SA 22	1896
Vigilant	A 534	1902
Valencia	GY 206	Not known
Victoria	SH 268	1912
White Pioneer	NE 3	Not known
William Hallet	LO 353	1919
William Ivey	LO 455	1918

A 412 *Dorileen* beached in the Tyne in 1920.

North Shields registered trawlers now just a memory

SN 100 *Ben Torc* sailing passed Knotts Flats, Tynemouth.

The stern trawler SN 137 *Ben Idris* on the day of her trials.

Memories from Tom Bailey

Thomas Bailey has recently retired on Merseyside after fifty years association with the sea commencing with an apprenticeship at Wallsend Slipway, eighteen years at sea as a Chief Engineer and employment ashore with various companies. His father spent some time on North Shields trawlers but one trip was enough for Tom. This is his story.

In 1953 I made a 12 day trip with my father-in-law, Henry (Harry) Goodinson, who was employed on North Shields trawlers from a boy right through to skipper on board the *Judith Purdy* (A 220) and I can well remember the conditions on board as being absolutely primitive. I slept on a 'donkey's breakfast' i.e. straw mattress, in the forecastle with the crew, and despite being in the summer we 'dodged' a NE gale for about three days in the lee of the Farne Islands. I also remember the food on board being very minimal for the first two days or so whilst steaming out to the fishing grounds as the Cook, along with the majority of the crew, was recovering from two days of leave, no doubt with a great deal of the time imbibing of good local ale.

A 220 *Judith Purdy* with the *Earl of Buchan* in the background.

However once fishing commenced four substantial meals a day were produced irrespective of the weather conditions. The working conditions for all hands were quite unbelievable with long hours on deck and sleep taken only when all net hauling and fish gutting was completed and in between hauls. They slept in working clothes, sea boots and oilskins being removed only when turning in. Washing was generally minimal during the trip and from a bucket of hot water in the engine room just before berthing after twelve days. I can also remember receiving my 'fry' in a bass bag (straw).

Harry took the *Amerique* away fairly soon after her purchase by Purdy and I remember him telling me about the lack of stability and that she was in general a 'dog' of a boat to sail in and fish. Her problems were well versed and I can recall Mr John Purdy (Jnr), who was I believe a navel architect, carrying out various trials to remedy the problems of stability and fuel consumption. He also was later involved with the Ranger Fishing Company.

With the demise of the steam trawlers the requirements for trawler men of the old school was diminishing fairly rapidly and Harry came ashore for a spell. However that lasted only some two or three years. He then had a spell with Boston Fisheries and skippered stern trawlers out of North Shields. It was about then that I think he conceded that his era of fishing was about over with new methods and sophisticated factory vessels taking over.

Harry had been at sea most of his working life but had seen nothing of the world so he joined a local shipping company, the Stag Line, whose offices used to be on the bank top. He sailed with them as third officer (his skipper's ticket was not valid on deep sea ships) to Canada and various other places and enjoyed what he called a leisurely life working four hours on and eight hours off, unheard of in trawlers.

The North Sea was beginning to see oil and gas production and Harry together with many other North Shields trawler men sailed on stern trawlers that were converted to carry out rig stand by duties. Harry was alternative skipper/mate on a vessel the *Hector Gannet* when she capsized and sank off Lowestoft in 1968 whilst attending to an emergency on a gas rig. Harry together with two other crewmembers was lost in this tragedy. I believe that all of the crew was from North Shields and that the other skipper was Lionel Tomlinson, a member of another well-known fishing family from North Shields.

I Didn't Think Catching Fish Would Give Me
A Criminal Record

In July 1963 an excited Bob Dixon set sail as an apprentice on his
first fishing trip aboard the SN 49 *Dorade*, a 250-ton trawler
owned by Boston Deep Sea Fisheries. The trip was scheduled for
seventeen days. The trawler carried a crew of thirteen, nine of
who were from North Shields, the remainder from Hartlepool.
Their destination was Iceland but for Bob, who was fifteen years
old, this was to be no ordinary trip. In fact he was to contact
home some eight days after he sailed away from the Fish Quay to
tell his parents that he had been arrested. The North Shields men
were:

> Harry McKenzie, Mate of Cartington Terrace.
> George Lowther, Third Hand, Linskill Street.
> Norman Robson, Chief Engineer, Cherrytree Road.
> J. Redman. Second Engineer, Trinity Buildings.
> Ernie Barber, Deck Hand, Peartree Crescent.
> E. Harthill, Deck Hand, Elmwood Road.
> Herbie Grant, Cook, Beach Grove.
> Jimmy Flett, Apprentice, Rowan Avenue.
> Bob Dixon, Apprentice, Wark Avenue.

Some of the crew of the *Dorade*.

This was a period when relations between Iceland and Great Britain were strained and the 'Cod Wars' were at their height.

The *Dorade* had been fishing just outside the twelve-mile limit imposed by Iceland with other fishing boats and they were being shadowed and harassed by the Icelandic gunboats that were aggressively enforcing the twelve-mile limit. The *Dorade* became snared with another trawler and both vessels drifted inside the Icelandic imposed fishing limit.

The skipper of the *Dorade*, Alan Woods from Hartlepool, saw the Icelandic gunboat racing towards them and frantically tried to haul in his fishing gear in order to escape. Bob and the crew strained to stow the gear but the odds were stacked against them. With the gear down the trawler could only make four knots and was no match against the Icelandic gunboats with their top speed of twenty-five knots. A boarding party swarmed aboard the *Dorade* as the gunboat *Odinn* pulled alongside and arrested the crew and the vessel. The *Dorade* was taken into Seydisfjordur where she was detained for ten days with an armed guard on board to prevent her escape.

Feelings were running high and Skipper Woods had no confidence that he would have a fair hearing. He was found guilty of illegal fishing and fined £2,166 and his gear and catch, worth £1,760 were confiscated. The skipper was to describe the court proceedings as 'farcical' and claimed 'I was convicted before I went in.'

Upon release the *Dorade* returned to the fishing grounds and finally returned to North Shields thirty-two days later to a rousing reception. For a fifteen year old this had been some trip and certainly not what he had expected. He thought he was going to be a fisherman, but returned a convicted felon, well in Iceland anyway. Still it made for a good story and over the years his fine has been repaid in free beer.

THE FISH QUAY, UNION STREET AND BELL STREET

A fisherman with a sample of his catch. Two North Shields steam trawlers belonging to Robert Hastie are in the background.

As you walk onto the Fish Quay from Union Road, provided you do not fall in, you will come to the part of the dock which is closed off and which allows safe anchorage for the cobles and the remaining North Shields fleet of fishing boats. The current Fish Quay foundations were constructed in 1870 but the previous construction was not that far different from today.

Before the present construction a streamlet, which rises in Northumberland Park, used to flow into the river and was named the Pow Burn. The name Pow was a derivative of the Celtic word 'pwl' which means stream. The stream still enters the river here but through a culvert and is hidden from view. This area is now more commonly known as the Gut.

The Gut at North Shields Fish Quay, now a safe anchorage for the few remaining cobles fishing out of North Shields.

Near to this spot just up river, near the confines of the Fish Quay, is a deep-water moorage known as 'Peggy's Hole'. Because of its large community of seamen and its reputation for skilled boat men (being very skilful at steering their square-rigged ships in the confines of the crowded river), North Shields was a favourite field of operation for the much feared press-gang. During the French wars naval frigates frequently lay at anchor in this area, partly to protect the port and partly to make impressments for the navy.

One of the naval vessels involved in such press gang raids was the naval frigate *Peggy*. On 6th February 1765 this sloop of war sailed into harbour and anchored in the deep pool close to Pow Burn, this place was an oft-used place for ships that lay in wait for a good tide. The *Peggy* was well known for using press gangs for use in the French Wars and the deep pool would take on the new name of 'Peggy's Hole'.

It is suggested that on this occasion the *Peggy* press-ganged a number of Tyne pilots into naval service but these men were made of sterner stuff. Shortly after the *Peggy* cleared the harbour bar the press-ganged men overwhelmed their captors and docked at Scarborough where they regained their freedom and returned home to the River Tyne.

As more battles were fought at sea rather than on land at this time North Shields was particularly prone to press gang raids. On 26th April 1793, a few months after another war started with France, troops from the Tynemouth garrison took the exceptional precaution of drawing a cordon round North Shields, while the press-gangs from warships in the harbour rounded up no less than 250 seamen, mechanics, labourers and men of every description and forced them on board. No wonder that in 1796, and again in 1815 and 1819, there were serious disturbances at Shields provoked by seamen. There are many local songs, some dating from the later eighteenth century, about the activities of the press-gangs particularly that of the notorious Captain Bover.

The Shieldsmen would provide great use during this period and those who did not sign up willingly were soon press-ganged to do so. This would then add additional burdens on the town of North Shields, as once a man had been unwillingly pressed into naval service, his family would have to rely on the local parish for support. Indeed the poor rate in Shields with its large community of seamen and boatmen would rapidly increase following press-gang raids.

Union Road may be mistaken as containing many of the original buildings of old North Shields but sadly this is not the case. The oldest building on the north side of this block opposite the Fish Quay sheds is the premises of William Wights Grocers and Ships Victualler. These premises have operated as a shop and local meeting place since 1929. The premises were formerly the Highlander Hotel and the interior of the shop still retains many of the original bar fittings.

Step inside the shop for a minute or two and prepare to be transported back to a forgotten age where personal service was the order of the day and there was no reason to rush or hurry. This shop is as much about being a working museum as it is a business but there are hidden treasures like old fashioned liquorice sweets and jelly babies, hand rolled bacon and black pudding which has not been neutralised by Brussels bureaucrats, sherbet dips and sour plum boiled sweets. As you wander around with your taste buds salivating look for the sign the 'Cabbage Patch'. To those in the know this is as famous a place on the Fish Quay as the lighthouses.

The fishing community both at sea and ashore has always had a reputation for working hard and playing hard. Playing hard was a euphemism for taking to the 'demon drink' or 'liquid laughter'. For such men there are no normal times to have a drink. They are not restricted by the time of the day, the sensibilities of other people or convention. If they have been working hard throughout the night or have just docked the justices licensing laws did not apply to them. The Cabbage Patch was the North Shields equivalent of a 'shabine' – an unlawful drinking den but it served an immense social purpose. William Wights grocers opened every day at 8am and so did the Cabbage Patch. Drink, mainly beer and whisky, was bought across the counter in the shop and then consumed within the confines of the Cabbage Patch along with some of your friends, work colleagues, local and river police. There they would stay until the local pubs opened or until a trawler owner or his representative, known as a ship's husband, went looking for a crew. They knew they were guaranteed to find willing, if not exactly able men, at any time of the day. Once at sea they quickly sobered up. And why was it called the Cabbage Patch? – for the simple reason that the room was the vegetable store and everyone sat around on the cabbages that they would eventually cook once they were at sea. It gives a new meaning to being 'cabbaged'.

The doorway to the infamous Cabbage Patch.

Alfie Walker was a regular at the Cabbage Patch and like many fishermen one of the hardest drinking sessions was just before they sailed. This was the last drink for some time and had to be enjoyed to the full. It also gave the crew some dutch courage if it was blowing a gale or the weather forecast was bad. However on one occasion it was not the Cabbage Patch but the lounge of the New Dolphin Inn that was to be his downfall. Alfie had just been promoted to third hand on board

GN 70 *Mary Ann Purdy* and the crew assembled in the New Dolphin one Saturday morning before an afternoon sailing. Unfortunately drink got the better of them when they discovered that Scottish and Newcastle Breweries were having a promotion in the pub and for every photograph they took a free round of drinks was provided. The crew became instantly photogenic and many photographs were taken. By the time that the ship's husband arrived to whip the crew into shape they were all drunk and past caring. The whole crew were immediately sacked and Alfie blamed for the affair. The following Monday the whole of the crew was re-instated and sailed for the fishing grounds. It would take another trip before Alfie was promoted back to third hand. Apparently the leniency shown to the men was helped by the fact that the brewery contacted the ship's owner and explained that it was their fault that they had got the crew drunk. Some monetary recompense was made and everyone was happy. Scottish and Newcastle Breweries recorded this mild form of mutiny for posterity.

The crew of the *Mary Ann Purdy* who failed to sail. Left to right: Harry Bailey (Fireman), 'Darky' Anderson (Chief Engineer on the *Lynn Purdy*), Hector Mackey (Fireman), John Duff (Deckie), Aida the barmaid, Ronnie 'Mopsy' Reynolds (Deckie) and Alfie Taylor (Third Hand).

Victorian concern that pauper children would become the future thieves and rogues of British society led to the Industrial Schools Act of 1866. Schools and training ships were established; part funded by the government and part by private donations, to provide training and education for homeless and destitute boys (not convicted of crime). The act sought to assist boys who were in danger of becoming destitute and homeless through parental neglect, poverty or by becoming orphans. Left to their own devices undoubtedly these boys would have embarked on a life of crime and society was aware of this.

It is important to be aware of the national background of these training ships. Britain, 'the workshop of the world', was at the height of her commercial and imperial power in the 19th century. There had been considerable growth in all forms of shipping but the number of her seamen had not increased in proportion to the demand. Here was a chance to train future seamen from an early age and to also tackle the serious crime problem by such boys.

On 17th January 1868 the Admiralty placed the frigate *Diana* at the service of the society, which had been formed to help these boys. She was moored in the river off the Fish Quay but was quickly replaced by the *Wellesley*. This ship had been an old line-of-battle ship, the *Boscaipen*. By the 1870s, in her role as a training ship, she was moored off North Shields.

Routine on board the training ship was harsh. At four thirty in the morning in the summer, or at five in the morning in the winter, the hands would arise, wash, breakfast, and clean the decks. At seven thirty in summer, or eight in winter, there were divisions for inspection, followed at eight thirty by prayers, then instruction until eleven thirty. The boys were allowed thirty minutes free time before dinner, which was served at noon. Further instruction then followed again from one until three thirty in the afternoon, then drill or singing. Supper was served at four thirty, play, then prayer, and to bed at seven thirty in the evening, except when there was a night school or reading room party, which allowed the boys to retire to bed an hour later.

The *Wellesley* was destroyed by fire in March 1914 but such was the quality of their training that all the boys escaped without harm. The boys were eventually moved to a permanent home in the Royal Naval Barracks on the sea front at Blyth.

The *Wellesley* Training Ship, destroyed by fire on 11th March 1914 with no loss of life. The background shows the maze of housing crowding in on the Fish Quay.

Images of Days Long Gone

Sorting fish
outside of
Kinnear and
Co Fish
Salesman,
Union Quay
at the turn of
the century.

None fresher
than when
caught today.

Replenishing the lighting system on board a trawler with Anglo-American Lamp Oil.

Always something to be seen amongst the crowded fishing boats.

Liddell Street and Clive Street

Looking down on Clive Street from the bank top of Yeoman Street.

Liddell Street and Clive Street are two quite short streets. Liddell Street was named after Henry Thomas Liddell, the Earl of Ravensworth and starts as we walk west towards the Ferry Landing just past the Ice factory on the Fish Quay. This street ends at the bottom of Lower Bedford Street, which was also known as Wooden Bridge Bank.

Custom House Quay can still be found at the beginning Liddell Street where the Wooden Dollies have stood for centuries. Here the Press Gang had its headquarters and many of the local sail makers.

Liddell Street, 1933 looking west.

Today as we pass by the redundant dry dock between the two phases of the Dolphin Quays we enter Clive Street, a street of paradoxes where all that was bad in society was on immediate view to the rich merchants, shipowners, captains and entrepreneurs who frequented this street. Clive Street may have been named after the wife of Hugh, Duke of Northumberland but other bodies of thought believe that the name was a corruption of 'cleaver', a tool in frequent use in the many butchers shops that once occupied this street. In 1848 there were 18 such shops in this small street, the most famous being Thomas Ratcliffe's who supplied all the meat for the army, the navy and most if not all of the North Shields Whaling Fleet. As many as eighteen bullocks could be seen hanging outside Ratcliffe's shop, each weighing up to one hundred stone and there was another fifty-one butchers shops in the township.

The junction between Liddell Street and Lower Bedford Street, *circa* 1933.

The Seven Stars Public House stood at the bottom of Lower Bedford Street where it joined Liddell Street. The site is opposite the redundant dry dock situated between the two phases of the Dolphin Quays housing complex.

Doctor Marr had a shop in Clive Street that looked like a chemists but the brass plate on the door announced that Doctor Marr was a Surgeon and an Accoucheur. From his surgery/shop he would sell pills, an ounce of castor oil, or even a pennyworth of salts. In his shop window there was a display of poppy heads (opium was on general sale in those days), camomile flowers, a sheet of soap or sticking plaster, a truss, a skull or two, two or three bones, an artificial hand, two or three lancets and a dishful of teeth. Obviously Doctor Marr's was a one-stop shop.

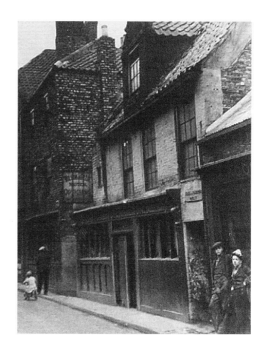

The Star and Garter Inn on Clive Street could trace its origins back to Tudor times. Two likely looking characters appear to be idling their time outside.

One of the worst areas was an alleyway running from Clive Street, along the Quayside, up to Yeoman Street. It was known as the Dark Stairs. In 1855, the *Shields Daily News* echoed the views of the respectable residents when it called for these properties to be demolished, referring to them as the 'refuge of the lowest dregs of society'. The newspaper asked, 'Who can estimate the amount of immoral conversation that passes, the unlawful schemes plotted, or the low, filthy literature read in common lodging houses and the intemperance that prevails in this nest of vice?'

One colourful court case tells how one prostitute, called Elisabeth Robson, lured a fifteen-year-old sailor back to lodgings in Clive Street and, in the morning, made off with his uniform. The scantily clad lad called in the police and Robson was caught. She was sentenced to one month in jail having 'been nine times in the house of correction'. It would appear that its name did not live up to reality.

Despite the plethora of public houses in the area there was still a need for non-alcoholic refreshment such as Dandelion and Burdoch, Sarsaparilla and non-alcoholic herb beer. This establishment was in Charlotte Street.

NEW QUAY, DUKE STREET AND THE BULL RING

The New Quay looking west towards Smith's Docks. The Crane Hotel is now known as the Chainlocker.

The short street that runs from the bottom of Borough Bank, from the Port Hole Public House (formerly the Golden Fleece) to the derelict area of what was once the largest ship repair yard in the world, Smith's Docks and Engineering, is known as New Quay and Duke Street.

Borough Road or Borough Bank as it is locally known was constructed by the North Eastern Railway Company to join the Railway Station to the Low Town. This undertaking required a deep cutting to be made to join up the old town with the new town. This steep hill accounted for more than its share of tragedies.

The last tram in the region rumbled and trundled off into the history books in 1952 after more than half a century of service to the public. More than one company who tried to provide a tram service for North Shields disappeared into bankruptcy but by 1890 North Shields and Tynemouth District Tramways Ltd had established itself.

Tram lines clearly visible on the approach to Borough Bank from the town centre beside the Ballarat Hotel. Hopefully the next tram made it safely to the bottom of the bank.

North Shields had been for some time a cosmopolitan society where many people from different countries and religions had settled. On the edge of the New Quay at North Shields, not far from the ferry landing and the tram terminus stood a large wooden shed. This was Contasto's Café, which was run by a Greek family called Dianunti, where port workers, tramway men, shipyard workers and passengers waiting for the Shields ferry would stop for a cup of tea and something to eat. Running a café turned out to be a dangerous occupation for this Greek family.

It was on a Saturday evening on 27th September 1919 and Contasto Dianunti was washing the last cups in the back room before closing down for the day. He had managed to come through the Great War unscathed but peacetime for Contasto was to prove more dangerous on more than one occasion. Suddenly there was the most deafening crash and Contasto was thrown to the floor. He was aware of wood splintering and the tearing of floorboards as the shed was torn from its foundations. His precious café was pushed towards the quay, stopping only a few feet from the edge.

Contasto picked himself off the floor and clambered out of the wreckage without injury to find the number thirteen tramcar leaning against the remains of his café.

Trams No 16 and 12 in Howard Street. The one on the left is bound for the New Quay.

Initially this tram route, when it opened in 1901, was only allowed to run single deck trams but this restriction had been withdrawn in favour of two brakemen. Eventually this restriction was lifted when it was considered that the motormen had sufficient experience. Contasto's café was rebuilt in the same location and the cups of hot steaming tea flowed once again.

Thirteen years later, tramcar number thirteen again ran away down the bank. On this occasion it seems that when turning from Saville Street into Borough Bank the wheels had locked and the tramcar had started to slide down the steep bank. The motorman had tried vainly to stop the car, which almost overturned on the sharp right-handed curve at the end of the hill by the Golden Fleece public house, and would probably have done so had it not been for Contasto's café. It would seem that there was a compulsory stop on Saville Street as the line turned down towards Borough Road but the motorman had approached the compulsory stop at too high a speed, and had locked his wheels in endeavouring to pull up.

Once again Contasto's café had saved the day and on this occasion the café had been empty. It is suggested that despite the motorman being adjudged as negligent and having caused this accident that employees pointed out that thirteen was not the luckiest of numbers, whereupon the offending tramcar was given the number eleven when one of the old single deck cars was scrapped.

A modern day view of where Contasto's café used to be which is believed to be where the white van is parked.

Almost two years later, on Sunday evening the 31st July 1921, under almost identical conditions, tramcar number twelve ran away when descending the bank with tragic results. Like number thirteen in 1919, it derailed on the curve, the wheels ploughing furrows in the stone cobbles as it jolted towards the river. Fortunately Contasto's café was again closed, but it took the full force of the impact, which moved the café once again towards the river. Fortunately the tramcar was deflected away from the river but with an ear rending smash, that made the ground shake, the tram fell on its side, throwing the top deck passengers off the tram onto the cobbled quay. The toll this time was five dead and thirty-two injured, some seriously.

An enquiry found both the brakeman and the motorman to blame. A fixed speed limit on the bank of four miles per hour, more thorough training for motormen and conductors and an improvement in the braking system of the tramcars was instigated. From then on there were no more incidents of runaway tramcars. Contasto Dianunti was now allowed to serve his cups of tea in peace.

The Bull Ring lies to the side of the Crane House Hotel (now named The Chainlocker) and is now a bus terminus. However this area goes back into antiquity to a time when the inhabitants of North Shields indulged in the popular sport of bull baiting.

The Golden Fleece Public House was at the opposite end of New Quay to the Bull Ring. The picture must have been taken after 1925 which is when police boxes were introduced.

With the growth of the fishing industry came the seedier side of life, and by 1878 police records showed that some 301 known prostitutes lived in Shields plying their trade around the many pubs, in fact, at one point in our history a one quarter mile stretch had some 50 inns and public-houses, many of which were dens of infamy. Perhaps the most grand, was the stone built Northumberland Arms on the New Quay, across the road from the Shields Ferry Landing, now converted into flats and called Collingwood Mansions.

The Northumberland Arms was not a place for a family night out and had a reputation as a rough place but it was one of only two places with a drinking licence with late night closing at weekends. Everyone knew of it as 'the Jungle'. Most of the criminals of North Shields could be found there where they used it as a meeting place for doing various illegal trades. Many of the local prostitutes could be found there 'looking for business' or a 'short time' and although most of these women could not classed as good looking or models they nevertheless kept themselves busy making a living. Many were known by nicknames such as 'Big Scotch Christine', 'Molly X', 'Irish Agie', 'Jinny the Vamp', 'Coal House Lil', 'Scotch Mary', 'Cock Eyed Ester' and 'the Chancer'. The Northumberland Arms was known throughout the world and was used as a regular pit stop by sailors and fishermen.

Joseph Ackerly used to frequent the Jungle and many more of the local pubs in the area. Josie, as he was known, was unashamedly homosexual and he was the North Shields equivalent of the naked civil servant. Times were different with no political correctness and everyone knew him as 'Josie the poof' or 'Josie the Fish Quay Fairy'. Josie was proud of his sexual predilections. He wore his homosexuality like a badge of office and was liked by everyone. He was not the only openly gay male to frequent the area as there were others known as Della and Debbie.

The building on the left later become the infamous 'Jungle' – the Northumberland Arms.

Josie worked in the local kipper factory for 34 years and was reputedly such a hard worker that he could put two women to shame such was his work rate. The days were long. Josie frequently started as dawn broke and would not finish until after 7pm and then it was off to the pubs wearing his kipper perfume. Josie's forearms were constantly the colour of kipper juice. One day Josie was seen sporting a very nice shade of hair colouring. There are various stories surrounding how Josie came to dye his hair but he insists that he did it of his own volition. Others would have you believe that Scottish sailors or matelots, who Josie had befriended and had desires on their bodies, played a cruel joke on him and upended him in the kipper barrel but Josie will have none of this for one very good reason. Josie intentionally died his hair, or what was left of it, but he forgot to fully immerse his head in the pungent ginger kipper juice. His hair turned out to be a rather fetching shade of reddish orange but his eyebrows remained their original colour.

CROSSING THE TYNE

The ferryboat *Northumbrian* navigates through the big freeze of 1963.

As we watch the North Shields – South Shields ferries hustle and bustle across the river with the regularity of a metronome it is easy to forget that until comparatively recently this was the only way of crossing between both towns without having to drive through Newcastle to access the first available bridge crossing. Before the Tyne Tunnel was opened, the three ferryboats then in operation, *South Shields*, *Tynemouth* and *Northumbrian*, carried about 400,000 cars each year as well as countless pedestrians. The opening of the Tyne Tunnel in 1967 brought about a significant drop in ferry traffic and the service was rationalised to carry only foot passengers.

The area's river has always played an important role in the life of the North Shields and has done so for a very long time. Historical documents indicate that as far back as 1377 there was a ferry service operating between North and South Shields.

River steamers could not compete with the faster electric trams and one by one the services were withdrawn as the companies went into liquidation. It was not until 1828 when the North Shields Ferry Co obtained a charter to operate a ferry service across the Tyne that the present day services, as we now know it, commenced operations.

To begin with there were three ferry boats: *Baron Newcastle*, *Durham* and *Northumberland*. Eventually the *Baron Newcastle* was replaced by *Tyne*. The North Shields Ferry Co was not the only ferry company to operate a service between North and South Shields. The Tyne Direct Ferry Co began a service in 1847 with a ferry called *Percy*; the Whitehill Point Ferry followed in 1856 with a ferry called *Favourite*.

In 1863 the Tyne Improvement Commission purchased the three ferry companies mentioned above and took over the ferryboats. In all the Tyne Improvement Commission had thirteen ferries built to its specification: *Shields* (1868), *Tyne* (1869), *Tynemouth* (1883), *J B Proctor* (1890), *Northumberland* and *Collingwood* (both 1896), *George Armstrong* (1904), *Thomas Richardson* (1906), *U A Ritson* (1906), *South Shields* (1911), *Durham* and *Tynemouth* (both 1925) and *Northumbrian* (1929). With no bridge downstream of Newcastle this ferry service was very busy

The ferryboat *Collingwood* leaving North Shields.

The horse and cart ferry at the landing.

The horse and cart ferry *Northumberland*, scene of a tragic accident.

Accidents to these ferries were not frequent but nevertheless they did happen. On 8th July 1875 at seven thirty in the morning the ferry *Northumberland* was crowded as she readied herself for the short trip to South Shields. A large horse drawn brewer's dray filled with casks of ale and spirits was on board. As the gangway was raised and the ferry turned into the river she took a list to one side and strenuous efforts were made to move the brewer's dray amidships but the drayman could not get the horses to move. The list grew worse and the dray slid backwards against the gangway, which burst open due to the weight of the dray and the horses. The horses panicked and strove to save themselves but the dray fell overboard dragging the horses with it. The horses sank at once together with the dray and were drowned. The bodies of the horses, the dray and most of its load were recovered later that day.

In 1929 there were eleven ferry routes across the Tyne between Newburn and the mouth of the river, but now only what was known as the Market Place Ferry survives as today's Shields Ferry.

The last passenger and vehicle carrying ferry was the steam-powered *Northumbria*. She had criss crossed the river tirelessly for 42 years but her final day came on 1st May 1972 when she was replaced by the *Freda Cunningham*, a brand-new £60,000 diesel boat built on the Tyne and run by the Tyne and Wear Passenger Transport Executive. Six days later, the *Northumbrian* took a nostalgic trip down river. For the crew, making a one-day comeback and for the 300 on board, it was be a sad day, a day to weep and a day to mourn.

The skipper was 62-year-old George Humble, a man who has been round the world on ships. On one of the last sailings he looked out from his bridge and surveyed the ferry he had worked on for the past 37 years. 'Would you feel sad?' he asked a journalist. It was almost an apology for the dingy black paint, the battered tyres hanging round the sides and the general air of not caring about appearance.

But everyone knew that George did care. He cared that he was two years and five months before he reached retiring age and he had hoped to spend that time on the *Northumbrian*. He cared because he had been the skipper for the past 23 years. He may not have cared too much about the wood and the metal, the fabric of the ferry, but he mourned the passing of a way of life – his way of life.

'Younger men were needed,' he told the press when he was asked about transferring to the *Freda Cunningham*, all blue and white paint, neat and pretty. Now skipper George Humble had no definite plans after Saturday. The day after that, the *Northumbrian* passed to the Tyne and Wear Passenger Transport Executive and that was the deadline for tender forms for its sale to he returned.

As premature retirement beckoned the *Northumbrian* remained special for George Humble. 'It's special to me because it used to speed me home at night after work from South Shields. It was the only link with the North shore when the last South Tyneside train had gone.'

For many a young boy and probably as many adults the ferry trips were exciting. Pushing through the stiff, noisy turnstile and then running down the jetty and onto the gently-rocking landing stage, passengers watched with bated breath as the great ferry berthed, the crew vigorously hauled on the ropes to pull her in, then the passengers would clamber onboard, the siren would blast, the engines started to throb, the signals would ring, then ropes were cast off, and the boat would slowly, very slowly, turn round and head into the river.

The ferry *Tynemouth*, withdrawn from service in 1968 after 43 years service.

Any late arrivals would be marooned on the floating stage, and the South Shields houses and docks would gradually seem to drift away; the ferry would reach mid-river, and a gale would be blowing from the sea. With just a bit of imagination on a clear and starry night the seven-minute trip was a little magical, if not exactly mysterious. Out on the top deck, the wind whipped in like a knife from the North Sea and the shipyard cranes bent over the silvery river like sleeping dragons nodding against the night sky.

The grimy dirty river scene hid behind the dark skirt of night whilst the lights of Tyneside cast a flattering glow. On the banks the busy shipyard floodlights played upon vessels from Oslo, Haifa, Rotterdam and Panama.

This was George Humble's life. Every quarter of an hour for half of his life he commanded the ferry *Northumbrian* on her trip back and forwards across the Tyne.

George went straight from the school to join his first ship for a three-month round trip to Buenos Aires. Then came seven more years of sleeping on a donkey's breakfast, a hessian sack full of straw, sailing round the world sometimes for ten months at a time.

However home ties began to pull and George left the oceans for a seven-minute stretch of the Tyne. That was back in 1935 in the days of the paddle ferry *Collingwood*, which landed at Comical Corner in South Shields and limped like a broken winged duck with one paddle out of the water when too many passengers crowded to one side.

These were the hey-days of the river link, dozens of women crossing to North Shields because the shopping was cheaper, hundreds of workmen heading for the shipyards, the horses and carts of traders and rag-and-bone men, the big dray wagons loaded with barrels of beer.

The drays were met on the North side by two horses called tracers, which helped pull the heavy load up Borough Bank, a lung bursting haul.

The car and passenger carrying ferry *Tynemouth* passes the passenger only ferry *U A Ritson* in mid river.

The last vehicular ferry, *Northumbrian*. On board is a Morris Minor van, a Morris van and a Morris or Austin 1100.

But the ferry's fate was finally settled on 19th October 1967, with one quick snip from a pair of scissors, the Queen opened the Tyne Tunnel and ferry passenger traffic dropped like a stone into the grimy Tyne.

This ferryboat service was taken over by Tyne and Wear Passenger Transport Executive on 1st May 1972. The ferryboats built to their order were: *Freda Cunningham* (1972), *Shieldsman* (1976) and *Pride of the Tyne* (1993), which are passenger only diesel ferries.

The *Freda Cunningham* failed to live up to the reputation of the *Northumbrian*, which she replaced. The ferry, plagued with mechanical troubles throughout her service, was taken out of service in 1993 and sold.

The two vessels currently in service between North and South Shields Ferry Landings, *Pride of the Tyne* and the *Shieldsman*, are of broadly similar design and dimensions although *Pride of the Tyne* is slightly larger. Both ends of the hull are identical, i.e. neither has a conventional 'bow' and 'stern', to make the best use of deck space for carrying passengers. The double-ended ferry operates diagonally across the river without the need for turning. This saves time, so the speed of the ferry can be reduced, saving wear and tear on the machinery and fuel without reducing frequency of the service.

One of the early paddle ferries approaching North Shields.

SMITH'S DOCKS, DOTWICK STREET AND BEYOND

The Docks of
The Largest Dry Dock Owners
and Shiprepairers in the World

Smith's Dock Company Limited

Docks at the North Shields Dockyard

Dock No. 4.   484 ft. × 68 ft.   Dock No. 5.   480 ft. × 68 ft.   Dock No. 6.   554 ft. × 71 ft.

Dock and Pontoons at the North Shields Dockyard

Dock No. 7.   298 ft. × 52 ft.   Pontoon No. 8.   335 ft. × 48.5 ft.   Pontoon No. 9.   430 ft. × 57 ft.

An advert for Smith's Docks from 1930.

75

We have now reached the end of our walk and before walking onto the ferry landing it is time to take a moment to stand at the entrance to Smith's Dock to try and remember despite its current dereliction what it was like when the Tyne was the shipbuilding capital of the world. Soon the area will be developed for housing but today, all of the dry docks still remain, sadly filled with rubbish and dirty water.

Smith's Dock was the largest ship-repairing yard in the world yet many people fail to remember Smith's when they think of the shipyards which made the Tyne great. They are more likely to remember the other great yards such as Swan Hunter's. It is perhaps not unnatural that the building of the great ships lingers longer in the public mind than the mending of the ships. The building of a ship is generally remembered and celebrated but of what passes between the birth and death they know nothing and would probably be surprised to learn that the repairing of ships is an industry almost as important as the building.

The entrance to Smith's Docks when shipbuilding on the Tyne was booming.

Scattered around our coasts there were innumerable yards, shops, and graving docks, each employing many hundreds of men, whose work, year in year out, is the refitting of vessels which have suffered accident in the course of their trading. Maintenance is also important and there was also the need for constant modification to meet the trading needs of the purpose for which the ships were built.

Work must be executed cheaply but it must also be done quickly, because every day a ship is in the repairers' hands means twenty-four hours earning power lost. It must be done well so that when the ship resumes her trading she can compete on equal terms with newer ships.

For almost a full century the North of England and the Tyne were described as 'The Home of Ship-Repairing'. Undoubtedly there were repairing centres earlier on the scene, for the industrial life of this great river was like the fishing industry a comparatively short one. In the 1850s the river was little more than a centre of commerce and a port, but during the following fifty years there was a huge increase in shipbuilding and allied trades upon the banks of the Tyne. Hundreds of thousands of jobs were created but today at the start of the twenty-first century shipbuilding and ship repairing on the Tyne is almost dead. The once busy docks are either derelict or the home for new marinas and riverside houses.

A modern day view from the back of the Crane Hotel looking down towards the ferry landing when Smith's Docks had long gone.

Whilst there were many firms on the Tyne which repaired ships, the one standing out most prominently was Smith's Dock Company Limited, an enterprise which carried on a very large business on both sides of the river at North Shields and South Shields.

The company, which was only formed in 1899, was in reality one of the oldest businesses of its kind in the Kingdom, having taken over the shipbuilding and ship-repairing undertakings formerly owned by Messrs Thomas and William Smith and Messrs H.S. Edwards and Sons. These were founded respectively in 1782 and 1768 and were carried on continuously by various members of the two families right down to the date of the formation of the Smith's Dock Company Limited.

At the height of its commercial strength in the first half of the twentieth century Smith's docked and repaired, on an average, nearly 1,000 vessels per annum, of a gross registered tonnage of over 2,000,000 tons. This yard alone dealt with nearly fifty per cent of the total number of vessels on the Tyne. Yet by 1998 Smith's Docks went, like many other yards, first into new ownership and then into receivership and abandonment.

The Italian cruiser *Piermonte* in the Bull Ring dock.

French four masted barques in Smith's Dry Dock.

Victorian terraced housing overlooked Smith's Docks and access to these streets, which are no longer there, was from the Bull Ring.

Dotwick Street ran from the Bull Ring up the bank and was like any other street of its time. But like much of North Shields it had a sinister side to it.

One of the most notorious and enduring stories surrounds the myth of 'Fifty Fafty's Ghost'. No one has been able to explain what Fifty Fafty stands for and the same legend is recounted in other sea faring towns and cities especially Liverpool. The ghost like many others may not be proven but the events of the legend are believed to be true. The majority of people of North Shields that lived along its riverside banks in the late eighteen hundreds were poor. One of the poorest families was Mr and Mrs Fafty whose married daughter lived next door. Various authors have recounted the story but I do not think that I could improve upon the following account written by William S. Garson, which was published long ago in the *Shields Hustler*.

'At the west-end of North Shields there was a house that stood in one of the old Courts off Dotwick Street – a place dreaded by all schoolboys – that was reported to be haunted by Fifty Fafty, and so gave Milburn Place a real ghost of its own.

The story was that Fifty Fafty's only son was apprenticed to the sea during the time of the French war, but before his indentures expired, he was taken by the press gang, placed on board the tender then lying at 'Peggy's Hole' and in due course sent into active service.

Looking down Dotwick Street towards the river where Fifty Fafty reputedly lived.

Years passed on, and the parents heard nothing of, or from their son, and when at last peace was proclaimed, he was forgotten by his townsmen and mourned as dead by his parents. In the course of time the daughter married and set up a house of her own a few doors away from that of her parents, who had now reached the declining years of their life.

One Christmas Eve a respectable looking man called at the daughter's house and introduced himself as her long lost brother. After satisfying her as to his identity, he informed her that after peace was proclaimed he went to one of the colonies, where by care and industry he had been enabled to save sufficient to secure himself against want, and to render the declining years of his parents peaceful and happy. They thought it would make a delightful Christmas surprise for the old people if they concealed the wanderer's identity until next morning, and so his sister took him along to Fifty Fafty's house, next door to the old Clarendon public house, and introduced him as a stranger who wanted lodgings for the night.

The old people received him kindly, and later in the evening he went to the public house next door, and brought back a bottle of rum and a bottle of whisky. After partaking of the contents of the bottles freely, the sailor showed his friends money and jewels, which he took from a bag fastened by a strap around his waist.

Late that night the sailor staggered upstairs to bed, and the old couple sat talking downstairs. 'I'm going upstairs to have that money,' said the old man. 'How?' asked his wife. 'Come with me to his bedroom and I'll let you see how.' When they entered the sailor's room the old man covered the face of the sailor, who was lying on the bed asleep, with the quilt and then lay with his full weight across the sailor's head.

After lying there some time, the old man stood up, removed the quilt, and said to his wife, 'He's as dead as a door nail, now for the money and the jewels.' He searched the dead man's pockets and found letters, photographs, money and jewels, which he wrapped in a piece of newspaper, saying, 'Come on and let's have a look at these things in the kitchen.' Once down stairs, the old man counted the money, while the old woman, after admiring the jewels, was looking at the photographs and letters.

Just then their daughter came into the kitchen by the back door. 'Tom is drunk again, mother, he abused me, so I'll stay here – what's those photographs and letters, mother – let's look?'

After examining them, their daughter exclaimed, 'My God, here's a letter from me to Harry, and this photo is of Harry, where is he now?'

'Upstairs, asleep, lass,' answered her mother.

'And here is a knife I gave Harry the first time he went to sea,' said the girl.

Just then the old man went upstairs and on returning to the kitchen, he said to his wife, 'The sailor's gone he must have gone without making any noise. Jessie, perhaps Tom will be all right when you go home tomorrow morning.'

When their daughter had retired the old man said, 'My God, have I murdered my own son, Jessie seems to think that it's Harry!'

'Yes, it's Harry, right enough,' the woman replied.

'Oh, my God, to think that we've killed our own son.'

'Keep your mouth shut, woman,' exclaimed her husband, 'we've got the money, and money means a lot to starving folk!'

Fifty Fafty is supposed to have suffered the extreme penalty of the law. His house, which was never again inhabited, was supposed to be haunted by the spirit of the murdered man for many years afterwards.

The tragedy took such a hold upon the imagination of the public that it was made the theme of a drama, which was very popular in the provinces in the early Victorian days.'

Other accounts say that immediately following his death the house became haunted. That very night of his death the ghost of the son returned, and every night thereafter when the clock struck midnight, the door hinges would creek, in spite of being locked. Then there entered a huge Newfoundland dog that would walk to each in turn, fondling with paws, laying its great head on the mother's knees; gazing up with soft melancholy eyes. The dog would then walk into the other room and rest at the foot of the bed on which the stranger met his cruel fate and stay until the first cock crowed, before dashing from the house howling as he passed. In this account the crime went unpunished but because of their guilt the Fafty's did not live long and had no time to enjoy their ill-gotten gains. The mother pined to death and the father died not long after. Before he died he unburdened his guilt and confessed to his son's murder. The dog would still be seen long after their deaths until the property was demolished.

The Wellington Vaults public house near to the Beehive Inn.

Near to the house of Fifty Fafty's legend stood the Beehive Inn where murder was committed. John Rutherford was the well-known licensee of the Beehive Inn and had married his second wife, Elizabeth Rutter at Holy Saviours Church, Tynemouth in April 1894. Following their marriage Elizabeth changed her name to Isabella Rutherford and joined John at the Tynemouth Lodge Hotel where he was the licensee.

John Rutherford, before he made a career in the licensing trade, had been a police constable in Newcastle City Police for eight years, a gaoler at Newcastle Gaol for 15 years and a Workhouse Master for 14 years. He became the licensee of the Beehive Inn shortly before the death of his wife.

On 20th February 1898 in the early hours of the morning John reported to the dock gateman of Edwards Shipbuilding Yard that he had found his wife badly beaten in the back lane of Dotwick Street and that he had carried her into the house. The police were summoned and found Isabella in one of the bedrooms of the Beehive Inn. She had been badly beaten about the face and head and was dead. Her husband John stated that following a domestic squabble she had left the house and only minutes later, hearing screams from the back lane he had found his wife lying unconscious.

The husband unfortunately and surprisingly because of his background did not understand the process of death. The police surgeon found Isabella in a state of rigour mortis. This condition does not occur for many hours until after death and he estimated the time of death as four to five hours prior to his examination. Other witnesses had reported a violent domestic going on between John and Isabella at around one o'clock that morning followed by a loud bang, some groaning and then silence. This proved conclusively that John was lying and was to be his undoing.

John Rutherford was immediately arrested and charged with the murder of his wife. He was lucky to escape the gallows, probably due to the fact that he had only beaten his wife, which almost accepted practice. He was swiftly convicted of the unlawful killing of his wife and transported to Australia on one of the convict ships.

Looking up Dotwick Street from the Bull Ring. The Beehive Inn is on the right beside the lamp post.

DO YOU KNOW THE FISH QUAY PC 7?

A young PC 7 Ken Banks.

The Fish Quay was there long before organised law enforcement was in operation in North Shields and at this time the Quay was a thriving centre of industry and crime! Indeed maybe it was because of the Quay and the activities which took place there, that it was found necessary to establish some form of system whereby property could be effectively protected and those who broke the law detected and punished. The history of the Fish Quay is of course very well documented and there is little need to repeat it here except to say that there is a correlation between it's history and crime, law enforcing and general disorder.

'Coppering' in the early days. Taken around 1890 the Inspector continues to wear the kepie whereas the Sergeant has moved to the more traditional helmet.

In the early days the town of North Shields was essentially the Fish Quay and its inhabitants. Tynemouth Village was a separate entity centred on the Priory and the Monks who industriously inhabited it. Preston and Chirton were concerned with the mining industry and New York and outlying areas were reliant on agriculture for their survival. It was many years later that the town of North Shields and the outlying districts combined with Tynemouth to form a Borough, indeed it was not until 1849 that a Royal Charter of Incorporation created the County Borough of Tynemouth.

Lawbreaking at the time of the early days of the Fish Quay was rife, and although not unique to the area, such was the extent of crime in the 'low town' that it was inadvisable to wander alone, especially at night, and that included the policemen! Offences varied in degree from petty theft to violent assault in such severity that the Larceny Act and the Offences Against the Persons Acts of 1861, together with the Vagrancy Act of 1824, might well have been compiled with the Fish Quay and the surrounding area in mind.

Most of the shipowners and men of substance and social standing had found accommodation in the original Dockwray Square which at the time was perhaps the most prestigious location in 'Shields' to be domiciled, for it stood in a prime position overlooking not only the river, but also the Quay where their financial interests lay.
Keeping watch on their property and their wares was no easy task because if property was broken into and goods stolen they were rapidly dispersed within the riverside dwellings, never to be seen again by the lawful owner.

This situation became a major problem for property owners and business men along the riverside and the consequence was the establishment of a small number of watchmen paid for by the businessmen of the town, the objective being to minimise pilfering. History seems to suggest that this was not the complete answer for several of the watchmen, whose duties also included lighting lamps and calling out the hour of the night, saw it as an ideal opportunity to pilfer for themselves with the minimum risk of being found out.

The problem persisted until 1791, when it occurred to those whose businesses were being affected by unlawful acts to band together and form a corporate entity with the sole aim of detecting and preventing crime, thus the Association for the Prosecution of Felons was formed to operate in North Shields and Tynemouth. The aim of the Society was met by each constituent member contributing to a central fund, which could be drawn upon to offer financial rewards for information leading to the arrest and conviction of offenders.

The Fish Quay 'Polis' was always regarded as a good beat and in the days of physical confrontation, if you could quickly establish with any miscreant on whose side the law was on, there was no better beat. There was always a fresh fish supper on offer and the odd glass of free ale. In 1828 the township of North Shields made provision to keep law and order by appointing a constable whose name was James Masterson with a lock up house situated at Crow Quay near to the Fish Quay. Like many policeman he was never to be found when he was wanted but fortunately for Constable Masterson, whose was known for some strange reason as Jenny, his wife could be equal to the occasion in keeping the law, if not the peace. It is reported that when a disturbance took place in Duke Street opposite the constables headquarters out rushed the heroic woman flourishing her lesser half's high authority and loudly proclaimed to the protagonists 'Peace in wor Jenny's name, for if wor Jenny's not at home, his staff is.' Peace was allegedly restored.

The Society lasted for 99 years, and in 1841 was joined by another similar organisation that seems to have identified the need for more incentives to convict the felons of the Town, presumably because of the widening of the Borough boundaries and the resultant population increase.

Apparently these two organisations worked together fighting crime long after the formation of the first official police force, the North Shields Police in 1830, until their disbandment some twenty years later on the first of January 1850, when the County Borough of Tynemouth Police was created. Seemingly the existence of the 'Prosecution of Felons Societies' was well received by the new constables, for they too received financial gain for apprehending wrongdoers, no doubt a useful source of 'topping up' their meagre pay. The Fish Quay becoming a veritable goldmine until 1890 when the respective Societies for Prosecuting Felons ceased to exist and responsibility was totally in the hands of the police, who by that time had proved their worth.

The Fish Quay 'polis', *circa* 1870, one of the earliest pictures known. The photograph unfortunately is not of the best quality but he is not holding a fish, just his gloves.

Maybe because of the incentives of the extra money, or mere enthusiasm for their task, the constables of Tynemouth Police executed their duties with zeal and were, in the early years, instrumental in bringing large numbers of Fish Quay thieves to justice. Whereas in other parts of the Borough crime varied, on the Fish Quay there was a ready source of larcenable material, namely fish, and varied and ingenious ways of stealing it were evolved over the years.

The zealous activities of the police however resulted in them becoming less than popular among the workers and residents of the overcrowded and slum areas of the 'Quay'. Indeed it was a dangerous place for the early police officer to be if care was not taken. In later years, although less dangerous, a new 'copper on the Quay' was treated with grave suspicion by many and exploited by a few.

In more modern times Kenneth Banks, who retired as a Police Sergeant, spent some time as the 'Fish Quay polis.' Ken is an authority on policing history and his story gives a cameo snapshot of some of his many experiences as a police officer.

Ken joined Tynemouth Borough Police in 1954 and at that time something of a metamorphism was taking place on the Fish Quay. Gradually the old slums were being demolished and with them a substantial amount of crime. The plethora of closely adjoining properties, which had housed and protected lawbreakers by the score, and which had evolved from the riverside stretching up the river banks to the developing town of North Shields were slowly but surely being eroded and uninhabitable even by those who had constantly sought shelter from the law in their warrens.

Ken paraded for duty one day to find that one of the regular Fish Quay PC's was going on leave and then on a course, which meant his duties had to be covered for a period of a few weeks. The regular officers jealously guarded the good postings and it must have been a wrench for one of them to leave such a prime beat in such hands as PC Banks.

'Do you know the Quay, number seven?' asked the Inspector. Seven was Ken's police number, generally referred to as a collar number despite the fact that the high collared tunics had long been consigned to the history books. 'Yes Sir, I know the Quay very well,' came the confident reply to the Inspector's question. Ken must have sounded convincing for he was then directed, not asked, to cover the Fish Quay beat during the absence of his colleague.

After all Ken reasoned, his father worked on the Quay for Hunter's Fish Merchants for several years, his grandfather had been Assistant Quay Master at one time, his uncle worked for Richard Irvin in the net factory, another uncle had had a fish merchants business on the Quay, and his son, Ken's cousin, worked there too. All this added up to multitudinous tales of 'The Quay', the truth of which PC Banks was to discover for himself in later years. Many happy hours of school holidays had been spent in exploration and discovery on the Quay, in many ways another world from the accustomed norm. An added bonus

One of Ken's former colleagues pictured here at the Fish Quay sheds keeping order in 1878.

was the fact that one of Ken's friends had a dad who wore a uniform and worked shifts at Lloyds Hailing Station, a good place to be for a couple of young schoolboys intent on adventure. What more was there to know?

The confidence of the response in answer to the Inspector's question however was to be quickly to be shattered. It took just a little while to realise just how wide of the mark his resolute answer had been. It quickly became apparent that his Fish Quay knowledge was somewhat limited, even vague in relation to what he was to learn whilst policing the Quay, and the task of instituting the learning process began in earnest!

Tynemouth Police Standing Orders was clear in its demands of the Fish Quay Constable in that they stated that no fish was to leave the market from it being landed until its sale the following morning, and in order to enforce this local bye law the policeman had to stand on the Quay from the commencement of fish landing at midnight, until relieved at six o'clock the following morning. On one particular night early into Ken's initiation on the Fish Quay a very good catch was landed from the many trawlers which operated from the Quay at the time. At about two in the morning, when the cold was beginning to bite and pangs of hunger were gnawing away, Ken was approached by a sympathetic worker on the Quay. They all had to have Corporation permits to be there so Ken reasoned that it was presumably all right when the worker said, 'You look caad, bonny laad, wiv just brewed a pot o' tea in the hut, come an' have some.' Ken needed no further prompting and quickly ensconced himself in the hut. The tea was hot and it was manna from heaven. It was just what was needed to restore some sort of sanity and equilibrium to a very young and very inexperienced and very cold copper. It was also the moment that the artful thieves had been waiting for, because more fish went missing during those ten minutes than the rest of the night!

A wiser PC Banks didn't fall for that one again, although many alternative ploys were used, like 'you better come quick someone's collapsed' or, 'there's going to be a bit o' bother at the other end of the Quay.' With experience he quickly learned how to handle each incident but it was always difficult to prove that the apparent beneficiary was part of the thieving.

No prizes for spotting the CID officers – they are in the bowler hats. In 1894 the detective strength was one Detective Sergeant and one Detective Constable.

The popularity of the policeman on the Fish Quay varied. In most cases the 'old hands' who had served for many years were appointed permanently to the Fish Quay beat, originally Beat Number eight which later became Beat Number fourteen.

The older constables knew the ropes well enough. They were keenly aware of the ploys used in stealing fish, like pushing it down the waders or wrapping it around the body to keep it hidden, the obvious discomfort was compensated for in terms of 'beer money', for which the stolen fish was sold. The old time 'coppers' quite often used to appear to ignore this, but at the end of the shift would approach the offender and make him strip thus revealing the stolen booty which had caused him a lot of cold discomfort during the night! This was readily accepted by those who chose to pilfer fish, being well aware of the perils involved, and when caught offered little resistance. They acknowledged and respected the Police Officer's methods, although today it might be a 'different kettle of fish' so to speak!

Tynemouth Police a little before PC Banks joined the force. No doubt the same deceptions were attempted upon them. Photograph believed to be around 1890.

When a new face in a police uniform appeared on the Quay this was often the signal for the less honest to rub their hands in anticipation, for they thought they could hoodwink the new copper with their schemes like throwing the stolen fish over the Quay wall to an accomplice who would hide it for later collection, or float a tied up fish box containing stolen fish in the river to be retrieved when no one was looking.

However it would wrong to suggest that all Fish Quay workers were dishonest. This was not so, for most were regular night shift unloading hands, who worked regularly for the trawler owners and were totally honest. The dishonest minority of usually casual hands naturally threw suspicion on the regulars.

The system of unloading fish was a traditional one. Each trawler owner landing at Shields Quay employed a representative on the Quayside to oversee the landing process. Men would queue up from about 11pm, just after the pubs had closed, waiting to be selected for work. Each trawler owner representative knew the regulars very well and they were usually the first to be chosen. Every potential fish porter was required to be in possession of a permit issued by the Council, for without it there was no chance of work.

Often, when the selection process was over, there were several men who were not required, usually casuals. This potentially presented a problem for, expecting to be out all night, they were at a loose end and used to hang around the quayside. Some acted as aides to those who were pilfering, by hiding themselves at the rear of the 'sheds', waiting for stolen fish to be passed over the wall to them so they might hide it.

One of the difficulties for the policeman in determining whether or not fish had been stolen was the system of 'fries'. Each trawler owner representative had the authority to give an agreed amount of fish to Quay workers and this was accompanied by a chit, officially a document of authorisation to remove fish from the Quay before the start of the market. Most recipients of the chit stuck by it and gratefully went home after a cold, wet and arduous night's work with pay in their pocket and a bit of tasty lemon sole for the family tea, but there were those who sought to exploit the system by altering details on the chit with the objective of obtaining more than their share. The world of simple larceny had become fraud.

Fish was landed at the Quay every night except Saturday, there being no Sunday market. Night duty on a Saturday for the Fish Quay policeman became a shift of contrasts. For the first two hours or so he coupled up with the New Quay officer, as happenings on that beat were very often eventful, especially when the Northumberland Arms turned out at closing time. Many seamen from visiting ships, for North Shields was a thriving port in those days, found their way to the New Quay to spend their accrued wages on drink during the evening and, as a consequence, their time in the police cells during the night. Fights abounded at closing time and it took the joint efforts of the two beat officers to control things. The Police van was often on standby in the area and was frequently needed. By contrast, just a few hundred yards away on the Fish Quay everything was relatively quiet. At about midnight, the Fish Quay constable would return to his beat and commence the laborious task of checking all business premises for insecure doors or unusual lights burning.

Although crimes involving breaking and entering did occur on the Fish Quay, it was minimal in comparison to the rest of the town area where most of the shops were situated. It was well known that it was pointless breaking into fish stores during the weekend as no money or valuables were kept on the premises. The only places worth the effort of burglary were the cafés and Wight's Grocery Store where there was likely to be something worth stealing.

Drunkenness on the Quay itself was a minor concern. Seamen whose vessels were tied to the Quay and who 'toured the town' presented few problems. By the time they had had their fill and returned to their respective boats all they wanted was sleep, However on the odd occasion where drunks were encountered, one had to be very careful in their handling, as it was all too easy for a drunken man to fall into the river, especially if involved in a scuffle. Tynemouth Borough officers were always aware of the availability of help from their colleagues on the River Tyne Police. Although not a 'Home Office' sponsored force like most of the land based forces, they could always be relied upon to assist the shore officers when needed. Indeed the River Tyne man on duty on the late night ferry was often called upon to help out at the Jungle when things got out of hand, or the beat men were occupied with 'lock-ups'.

The River Police were always very much in evidence in the Fish Quay area. Quite often on nights when they had finished examining the riverside property from their patrol boat, they would patrol the waters of the quay area and were very effective as a deterrent to those bent on lowering stolen fish into the water for later collection. Indeed many prosecutions were successfully brought to the Tynemouth Magistrates Court through the diligence of the 'River Men' who were able to observe from their boat what those on the shore could not see.

River Tyne Police Officers often assisted their shore-based colleagues and performed sterling service on the river until they became part of Northumbria Police.

Too often, because of excessive drink, high spirits or pure accident, and because of the nature of the Quay, people fell into the River Tyne. This obviously presented a serious problem, for it could be very difficult to effect a rescue in certain circumstances. If the occurrence happened during the night it was less likely for it to be noticed and therefore more likely for the unfortunate person to drown, particularly if the tide was running high. Victims were very often swept out to sea to be eventually washed up on the beaches of South Shields or Sunderland. Apparently, according to survivors, the sudden dousing into the icy water was more than enough to counter the soporific effects of drink, and they were able to effect their own rescue, depending where about on the Quay they fell into the water.

When, unfortunately, a person fell into the river and drowned a number of things could happen to them, apart from death that is. Sometimes they were brought to the shore fairly quickly, but usually, just as bodies from the Tyne ended up south of the river, bodies recovered from the Tyne often had entered the water at Cullercoats or

Whitley Bay, or even further north. It was almost inevitable that such bodies had been in the water for some time and were in an advanced state of decomposition, due in part to the content and composition of the water, but also because of the hundreds of crabs, which invaded and fed off a body. It was the unenviable and onerous task of the Fish Quay policeman to supervise, and be actively involved in the transfer from the water of a partially decomposed body into the Mortuary, or Morgue which stood on the east end of the Quay. This building was fairly modern in comparison to adjacent property, and comprised a 'laying out' slab, a washing trough and basin, and sufficient tools and instruments for an initial post-mortem examination, for in every case of sudden death, even though it was obvious what the cause was, nothing could be assumed and foul play could not be ruled out.

The Mortuary, or 'Deed Hoose' as it became known was supervised by a Council employee who was very well versed in the procedures and could be relied upon to co-operate fully with the local 'copper'. Because of its refrigerated interior, the Mortuary was an ideal place to store fish, lawfully obtained of course, until the Fish Quay workers' shift was over (and sometimes the polis'), and it was fresh ready to take home. Apparently it was also ideal for keeping beer cool for a hot day!

Identifying dead persons brought from the river could be an irksome and tiresome task. In few cases the deceased turned out to be a local person, usually the unfortunate victim was a fisherman who had misjudged his entry onto his boat after a night's drinking, and had fallen, often between two vessels. In most cases they turned out to be Scottish men who plied their trade from the Tyne, and were unaccustomed to the vagaries of the Quayside.

School holidays presented further problems for the police. The riverside acted as a magnet to children during the summer months and they travelled from far and wide to 'gaan ti the quay to dee some fishin'. Unfortunately the attraction of the water was too much. Some fell in and had to be pulled out, while others jumped in for a swim and soon got into difficulties. The fact that the offensive fish offal and the like floated in copious amounts on the water, the ever shifting tides and under currents made this a particularly dangerous place to swim and the general state of the polluted river had no effect upon the swimmers.

Long hot summer days, or so they seemed at the time, meant that children were reluctant to leave the Quay and this posed a problem for the policeman. After all protection of life was paramount in a Constable's oath taken when being sworn into office, protection of property came next. This necessitated a constant wary eye on the kids on the Quay. One just did not know what they would get up to next

The Fish Quay, by its very geographical structure afforded plenty of hiding places. Mention has already been made of the ways in which fish was concealed, but it was, and indeed still is ideal for youngsters' adventure games where concealment from 'the enemy' was so easily achieved. One could lie low for ages without discovery, and whereas this was useful for juvenile pranks, it also presented its dangers, for many of the old buildings were in a state of dereliction and, consequently very dangerous to play in.

The old buildings were excellent for hiding things, especially stolen property. Time and again when carrying out routine inspections the policeman would come across hidden treasure, the ill gained booty of some evilly disposed persons, just waiting to be collected! Some children were even in the habit of climbing the walls of the public houses, stealing crates of empty bottles (sometimes full ones), and hawking them round general dealers and off licences in the town, for each bottle was worth a penny!

In seafaring ports around the world there are to be found women willing to sell themselves for money – prostitutes. North Shields was no exception. These 'ladies' seldom, if ever, used their correct names, not at least until they were 'locked up' when actual names had to be used. They however revelled in a host of nom-de-plumes, or nicknames, and strangely they were always referred to by these names, as everyone was known by them. Such names as 'Molly X' (who hit Ken over the head with the high heel of her shoe during one fracas), 'Scotch Mary' and 'Scotch Jean', 'Welsh Betty', 'Aggie W' and 'Aggie G' to name but a few.

Most of the 'ladies' lived in the Fish Quay area or the 'Low Town', with access to the pubs and cafés virtually on their doorstep. In days gone by, the south side of Clive Street was a warren of pubs and cafés, all low class, downtrodden and literally dens of vice. Prostitution was rife as were offences of theft and violence, many a crime, even murder was planned and carried out in those ghettos during the late nineteenth and early twentieth century. Rumour has it that in at least one of the riverside flats a trapdoor construction was made under the flooring so that clients could be robbed and then expediently transported to the icy waters of the Tyne! The truth of this tale is in question, but like many rumours it is probably based on fact. If the unfortunate 'client' survived the river he was hardly likely to report the matter so the police of the day were rather limited in their actions. Fortunately the council carried out a programme of slum clearance and the inhabitants were scattered over a wider area.

When Ken joined the Force very few such dwellings of ill-repute remained, and the ladies, who tended to work for themselves, pimps at that time were very few in Shields, lived in close proximity to each other, often sharing accommodation in the region of the old Bells Flats in Liddell Street. On one occasion a queue of Chinese seamen formed outside one of the 'ladies' flats in more or less the same location as queues for the fish and chip shop form today to avail themselves of the illicit pleasures on offer!

Many derogatory terms have been used about the 'ladies of the town', and in some cases with total justification, for some could be quite callous in their general attitude and demeanour. Some would stop at nothing to cause personal injury as a means of retribution. One 'lady' during the course of her arrest for drunkenness took out a hatpin and actually stuck it in the policeman's eye. He didn't lose his sight in that eye but even today, some forty years on, he still shows the scar.

Most of the 'girls' kept themselves and their homes clean and tidy, in fact on such occasions when their homes had to be visited, one was always aware of their cleanliness. Many were very kind in their own way. 'Agnes' used to ply her trade and then go home to make her supper. It was her habit to make a bit extra so she could pop along to the police box with some refreshment for the night shift copper. Ken knows of no one who could vouch for the quality or taste of the food, but it frequently proved useful to feed the stray dogs in the station yard!

When Ken's late father-in-law was working for the corporation on cutting the grass banks on the riverside with his colleague one hot summer day, one of the 'girls', Rosie, came up to them with some cold drinks she had bought to help them cool off. Another 'Aggie W' used to call in to the police station at Christmas time with gifts for Ken's daughter (his wife was a policewoman and hence knew the girls well), of packets of sweets and dolls and the like, all of which she had bought as a genuine gesture of good will. Needless to say the Salvation Army Christmas Appeal benefited.

One of the less popular 'ladies', Marina, was something of a character. She would regularly ask one of the policewomen for 'a couple of bob' for a 'sit in' in one of the low town pubs. This of course enabled her to legitimately go into the pub and buy her first drink. The rest of the evening took care of itself! The day she decided to get married was an eventful one. Where the actual ceremony took place is anyone's guess, but the 'reception' was at the Alnwick Castle public house in the Town Centre one Saturday afternoon. The guests and the 'bridal pair' were seemingly well supplied with intoxicants with which to make a toast, for the whole place erupted in one gigantic fight that took several police officers quite a time and a lot of energy to quell. The cells were predictably full afterwards; the occupants included the

The Helmet Badge of a proud
and effective police force –
Tynemouth Borough Police,
1850-1969.

bridegroom and Marina who spent their wedding night behind bars (and not the type of bar the bride was used to).

Of all the beats in the County Borough of Tynemouth Police Force, there can be no doubt that number 14 beat, the Fish Quay, was the most varied. The different problems of the night have been described, fortunately the events did not happen every night, not simultaneously anyway! The only constant certainty of the hours of darkness was the usual 'sleepers out' on the quay. They weren't real vagrants as most could have gone home if they had wished. The Quay however held some sort of attraction for them and they were to be found sleeping in odd places, under fish boxes, on the backs of bogies and lorries and under the wide wooden beams of the Quay itself if the weather was clement. They did no harm, they scrounged their food and drink, they washed (occasionally) under one of the many taps on the quay, and made a dishonest 'bob' by acting as lookout for the fish stealers. One of them, 'Danny the Gulp' as he was known was quite extraordinary in that he could sleep out in the open in the most severe of weather and had a habit of swallowing small fish whole for his meals, or pints of beer in one gulp, hence his nickname. He thrived well, and lived to an old age, little the worse, or maybe the better, for his Spartan existence.

For PC Banks any of the shifts on the Quay could bring its share of experiences. One early shift, just before his finishing time of 2pm, he was making his way up Brew House bank towards his finishing point when he was overtaken by a particularly heavy-laden lorry labouring its way up the bank. As it attempted to turn left into Bird Street, a sharp bend with an evil canter, the inevitable happened. A loud crack signalled that the tailboard had given way and an avalanche of herring began to slide down the bank, gaining momentum as it proceeded, heading directly at Ken. There was no escape. Ken struggled to keep his feet as he fought his way in the opposite direction to the descending shoal! Fish engulfed his nether regions and managed to find its way into unmentionable places. Ken had to do something about it of course even though it was almost finishing time, and a rather embarrassed, red faced lorry driver's journey was delayed by a few hours while he tidied up the odorous, gooey fishy mess.

Ken went home that day alone. No one wished to be in his company. His feet slid around in his boots in fish offal and oil, his uniform an insult to one's olfactory senses. He was tired, hungry and just wished to get home, have a bath, a beer and an early night. At six o'clock the next morning of course, he was back on the Quay smelling sweeter than when he left it a few hours earlier.

As he started his new shift he recalled, 'What was the question the Inspector asked me seemingly so long ago, yet in fact was only a few weeks before.' Oh yes – 'Do you know the Fish Quay number seven?' I suspect his response by then would have been a rather more wiser and confident, 'Very well indeed Sir!'

I WAS THE LAST APPRENTICE AT THE 'HADDOCK SHOP'

Looking down on the 'Haddock Shop' from the bank top. The trawler *Glenesk* is in the centre of the picture and the square hulled ship is the training ship *Satellite*.

The Dolphin Quays apartment complex sits fairly and squarely on top of the site of an old shipyard that started life in 1822 under the name of Thomas Metcalf and Son. In 1899 with the birth of the steam propulsion it underwent a huge change and once again it was that small bunch of North Shields entrepreneurs, led by Richard Irvin, who were the catalyst for the change.

The Dolphins Quay housing complex overlooking the dry dock of the Haddock Shop.

Shields Engineering Company was formed later to be renamed Shields Dry Dock and Engineering Co Ltd. The company quickly became known as the Haddock Shop even when it was incorporated into Smith's Dock Co Ltd in 1954 because the company specialised in building and repairing steam trawlers.

Mike Ennis was he believes the last apprentice who worked at the Haddock Shop. The experience has lived with him all his adult life and this is his story in his own words.

This is the story about some of the men, not all of whom were sea going, but who were connected with ships, with whom I was privileged to serve my time as a fitter turner. Most of the men and all of the ships have now gone, along with the shipyards, and I feel that the world is a worse place for that.

I have always wanted to build and repair things to the extent that when I was young I was told to leave things alone. It was mainly clocks that I found fascinating and even now they still beat me when it comes to fixing them! We moved to South Shields when I was fourteen years old, which as far as I was concerned was the best move my mother ever made. The Tyne was always full of ships and I spent hour upon hour at the Mill Dam and the Ferry Landing just to be able to imagine what it was like to be on a ship.

Workers enjoying a rest at the Haddock Shop.

I joined the South Shields Model Engineering Society, run by Fred Whitehead who was to influence my engineering until the day he died in 1995. By now I had decided that I wanted to be an apprentice turner in the shipyards. Though I knew Fred quite well I did not realise that he worked at Smith's, and when I told him that I was to start at Smith's Docks in August 1957 I was told in no uncertain manner what I could expect from him. I was rather apprehensive but Fred was to become a great friend for the next 40 years.

Soon August 1957 came around and I was told to report to the time office at Smith's Docks. Smith's Docks was a large complex consisting of seven dry docks spread along a large part of the water front of North Shields.

At the Fish Quay, which was the most easterly part of Smith's, was a small dry dock known locally as the Haddock Shop. The firm of Shields Engineering had occupied this little dry dock and yard, which had been quite famous in the marine world as builders of small marine steam engines. In front of the dry dock stood a house where in the old days when sailing ships went there, the person who lived in that house was paid to have the bowsprit of the docked ship in her upstairs front bedroom window. In the winter this must have been a cold room. It was in this part of Smith's that I was to spend almost three years of my time and learn from some of the most accomplished men whom I was ever to meet in my life as an engineer.

Looking east along the quayside towards the Fish Quay.

The very unusually registered NE 3 *Mary White*. The NE registration denoted a vessel registered in Newcastle.

That first Monday at work came for a very excited though somewhat nervous sixteen year old. I had no need of an alarm clock; I was awake long before it started making that ungodly din. I had some breakfast and away I went to work, meeting Fred at the corner of our road. On reaching the Ferry all I could see were men. They were all over the place and they all seemed to be smoking. The ferry I caught was the seven o'clock and we were packed in like sardines in a can. I hesitantly reported to the duty time clerk, feeling very small and insignificant. I was made to feel welcome and within an hour I felt as though I had been there all my life. By the time I got home that night I felt like a grown man.

I started my apprenticeship in Burden's store in the Fitting Shop of the main yard, also known as the high yard, but what an awful place it was to start. It was dirty, it stank, and it was run by a man called Burden assisted by a one legged man called William O'Dowel, who had lost his leg in Burma in the last War.

In cold weather, starting work at Smith's was sometimes like Dante's Inferno. First thing in the morning the six steam cranes were getting up steam, along with the small tugs that Smith's operated. There were three of these small craft that were moored down at the old Baird's Dock next to the cranes. In addition all the heating fires were alight in the various sheds throughout the complex of Smith's. The effect of all this was a great pall of smoke, which combined with the other yards on the Tyne, along with tugs and ferries, must have made it nasty for people with bad chests.

Among the afflictions (other than Foremen) which apprentices had to endure, were some rather painful ones. The first of these I shall call by its universal name, 'Hammer Rash', which seemed to occur at a very early stage in one's working life, the cause of which was a 2lb piece of metal coming into contact with the hand holding a chisel. Another affliction was a very large blister which appeared on the palm of the hand holding a file or saw, and as we seemed to spend a great deal of time cutting one type of metal with another, these afflictions took a long time to heal, and were the cause of a good deal of mirth amongst the men in the shop.

They say it is hard growing up and for an apprentice fitter it was! I suppose it was worth it in the long run, though it did not help when your mother made you get undressed in the back yard because you were so dirty. The weather or the season made no difference. I was not allowed in the house until I was as nature had intended – scrubbed clean and lily white.

As I was approaching eighteen years old and about to work on ships Fred told me to request that I be allowed to finish my time at the Haddock Shop or Baird's dock. I went to see the Head Outside Foreman to request this, but he was none to pleased and made it plain that if I was allowed to move, the ships that I was likely to work on were small and I could end up losing valuable experience. I replied that I was aware of this but that I still wanted to go. I was told to go away and that he would think about it. Some days later he begrudgingly told me to report to the Haddock Shop. It was the best move I could have possibly made and for the next three years I was to be very happy.

The yard itself was small, the dry dock being only one hundred and eight-two feet long with a width of forty feet, and the quay length being not more than two hundred feet. However, in the small area that it covered, it contained all that had been needed to build ships, engines, and boilers. The machinery was old, the buildings had also seen better days, and in the winter the yard was full of draughts with water dripping from leaking roofs. As a consequence large heating fires were always in use when it was cold and wet, and these we were allowed to use to warm ourselves as long as you did not abuse the concession too much.

On arriving at the Haddock Shop, with my bait bag over one arm and my tool bag over the other I introduced myself to the foreman, Alec Craig. Alec, as was the custom with foremen, put me in my place and told me in no uncertain terms that I was there to work, go to College and not to fool around, and being in the Haddock Shop meant I would be put on trust a great deal. He then opened a hatch in the wall behind him and asked somebody to come into his office. Alec was too nice a man to be a foreman and immediately spoilt his stern, formal authority by introducing me to his charge hand calling me by my Christian name and stating that he was pleased to have me working with them. I never did see Alec loose his temper all the time I worked under him. I saw him worried plenty of times, and though I never did, it was easy to take advantage of him and some people did.

I was assigned to work with Douglas Scofield, and from the start Douglas (Doug) and I worked well together. I can honestly say that work became a real pleasure and that there were no such things as Monday morning blues. That first morning however was a culture shock. Going into the fitting shop I was astonished to find that all of the machine tools were belt driven. The equipment on which I was expected to work appeared to have come out of a Dickens novel. I could hardly believe my eyes. It was like stepping back in time, the only thing missing being gaslights, but on closer inspection I even found those! I stood there and thought to myself 'what have I done?' I was given the rest of the day to get myself sorted out and told to make myself known to all the people there. This did not take to long as the whole complex only had about thirty men working in it, and as I went around the yard I began to feel quite at home there, just as Alec had meant me to.

The next day Doug and I went on the trawler A 751 *Ben Gulvain* and that was another shock. She was filthy and when I had to get into the crank space in the engine room, I was confronted by one of the engineers' rice puddings, which he had not finished, and had just dumped into the engine crank space. I caught Doug looking at me out of the corner of his eye, expecting me to say something, but I said nothing and just carried on working. From that moment on we were mates and Doug on his part was to become a great teacher.

Doug had one very strict rule that I had to obey. This was that when going to work on a ship I carried the tools and he carried the acetylene light with its tube. This rule was never altered, and, if we had a labourer, he would be responsible for the lifting tackle. At times it must have looked like a master and his two slaves walking along the Fish Quay, but in truth we worked as a team, and the three of us each had a very specific task to carry out. Doug was responsible to Alec; I was to Doug and the labourer had to answer to Doug. A craftsman like that made sure his work was carried out. The labourer to whom I keep referring was a man whom Doug trusted and had worked with over many years. His name was Billy Taws, and to say that he was skilled in what he did would be an understatement.

To work in the Haddock Shop was like being in another world after the High Yard. Every tool seemed to be either old or worn and often it was both. The vessels too were old and worn out, and to me it felt rather special. I could relate to what the older men were saying when they used to talk about the work being done in the past.

The fact was that the Haddock Shop, along with Baird's, was built to make the type of engines being repaired on the tugs and trawlers, which at that time were still appearing. As long as they were coming Smith's allowed the small yards to stay open, but when the steam engines went, both the Haddock Shop and Baird's would be closed.

The *Lolist* in dry dock. Despite her Lowestoft registration she fished out of North Shields for many years. She was built at Middlesbrough in 1914.

However in 1959 the trawler and tug owners provided enough of their steam type of work to make money, and the way of life, with all the people associated with it, survived just long enough for me to be part of it. I was the last apprentice at these works but steam was finished when I came out of my time.

It was not all-hard work in the Haddock Shop and there were some distractions, quite pleasant distractions in fact. Opposite the shipyard was a grass bank that was behind the road. The grass grew long and luxurious on this little patch of greenery despite the pollution from all of the chimneys. This was the spot where the local girls took their boy friends in the warm summer afternoons, having had their fill of the local brew of Newcastle Brown or Exhibition ale. The girls would wave to us while they were being friendly with their new conquests! This always caused a great deal of laughter from us. If a ship had steam and was able to sound its whistle, or if the steam crane was at the dock and able to assist we knew we could have some fun of our own. The art was to pick the right time to sound the whistles. The noise was truly deafening and hopefully when the whistles sounded there were some coitus interuptus rather than an involuntary muscle spasm. Some of those men were so startled by the noise that they would try to run away at the same time pulling their trousers up. One of the girls always came up to us later when we were walking along on the quay and would always ask if that was a good show? The answer was always the same, 'not much detail'. She would then laugh and walk away saying something like 'Get the binoculars out next time.'

One other type of work undertaken by the Haddock Shop involved the local rope works and it always fell to the apprentices to carry out the repair work. The rope works were manned almost entirely by young women and they had a fearsome reputation. Apprentices went pale with fear when they were told that they were going to that place

The training ship *Satellite* was a familiar landmark moored just off the Haddock Shop for many years.

the next day. It was enough to make you go sick and as a result apprentices were not told they were going until the actual morning of the day because of the drop out rate. We only went about once a year, and as such had a fairly good idea when the time was due. We would do anything to get out of it. Self professed hard drinking and womanising nineteen and twenty year old apprentices would boast that it would be no trouble for them to go there, but when they came back they always vowed never to go there again!

The trouble with the place was the girls, their attitude to young men, and what to do with them when they could get their hands on them. They were sexual predators in the premier league. They thought it all a bit of fun but they ate apprentices for breakfast. I was very fortunate. When I went there the rope works were shut down for some reason and the girls had been laid off. When I say that I was relieved this was an understatement. Bob, an apprentice who worked with me, would volunteer for anything, and told Alec that on the next visit he would like to go. Alec grinned wryly and said that on next breakdown they had, he would be sent. He was and came back very much chastened and shell shocked as if he had been in the trenches during the Great War. I honestly think he was still blushing the next day but his lips were sealed. He was in a daze for the rest of the day. It was all meant in good fun on the girls' part, but to some of the boys at the time it was not pleasant. Sensibilities do not allow me to explain what went on but I think it would be true to attest that I am the better for not going through this form of sexual rite of passage. To apprentices who thought that being masculine was the answer, the old saying that 'the bigger they are, the harder they fall' just about summed the situation up. The girls always won!

There were two main trawler companies on the Quay whilst I was there, both using steam trawlers, all of which were very similar, having been made about 1914. The boats were registered at around two hundred gross tons, and were powered by steam reciprocating engines (triple expansion). Purdy, the first company which tried to keep its old trawlers in a fairly good state, ran a fleet of seven boats when I first started working on them in 1959. The hulls of their boats were painted green, the funnels black with one white band, all superstructures was brown and they looked very nice. Irvin trawlers on the other hand were running their boats down at this time, but in 1959 took delivery of their first diesel trawler, SN 40 *Ben Chourn*. By now the majority of their fleet was based in Aberdeen. North Shields at this time was supporting six of their steam trawlers which had black hulls, black funnels with two red bands on them, and brown superstructure. Another company, which had been famous in its day, was Robert Hastie who by 1959, were down to one boat, the SN 283 *William H Hastie*. She had a green hull, black funnel with a white H on a red band, and again brown topsides.

One week after I went to the Haddock Shop, I was sent to strip two boats prior to them being scrapped, A 362 *Sabina* and SN 42 *Kendale*

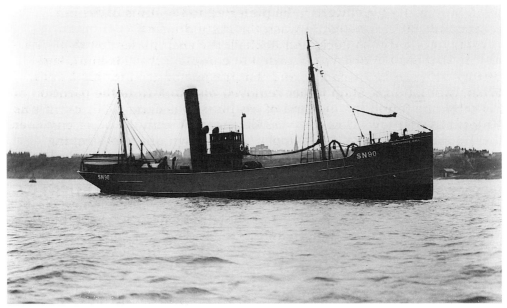

Vessels of the type depicted here in SN 90 *Nunthorpe Hall* kept the Haddock Shop in business longer than could ever be expected. This was due to the longevity of these tough steamers, which refused to die, and kept going when other modern machinery would have given up the ghost.

belonging to Tomlinson of North Shields. The *Kendale* for some reason was given a stay of execution, but she only lasted a few more months. She had acquired some fame, as she had started to take on water a few months before whilst tied up alongside at the quay, and after they had got her into dry dock and pumped her out, a bolt was found in her engine room bilge, which due to the motion of the ship, had rolled a hole in her shell plate causing her to leak. Her stern gland was leaking so much whilst she was at sea, that the engineer had not noticed this leak in the hull.

To say that the old trawlers were kept going on a wing and a prayer meant something at North Shields, and other places where old fishing boats were working out their useful life. However these boats were built tough and continued working when modern day machinery would have long given up the ghost.

Tugs and trawlers with wooden decks all had the problem of corroded steel plates under the wood, which as the boats only had a short life ahead of them, made it a rather expensive and uneconomical repair. The cure was thought to be simple, just drill a hole in the wooden deck and then pump in a non-setting mastic compound, most of the time this idea was more than acceptable. But on one trawler they pumped it around the engine and boiler rooms, which when they really got heated up, melted the compound. This then started to drip into the engine room, this was bad enough, but when it landed on a hot surface it started to smoke and smell. It was stated by the engineer that he thought that the leaks were to be preferred to the drips of the hot compound. At least he could wash the rusty drips off.

It was not only the decks that leaked, the shell plates did also! The engineer of SN 113 *Ben Vurie* started to complain that his bunk kept getting damp in bad weather, and that it was not good for his health. When the Haddock Shop joiner removed his bunk from the partition of his cabin, he found the foot end of his bunk was damp. This cabin was almost at water level down aft and he shared it with the other engineer, the mate and the cook. The skipper had his own quarters sleeping under the bridge. The cook's bunk, which was on the other side of the partition, was also damp though not as bad, the partition was used to give the chief engineer, and the mate small cabins, because of their rank. When the joiner pulled the partition down on the engineer's side he saw daylight through the shell plate, which up till then had been covered by the wooden framing of the partition. The wooden bunks were keeping the trawler watertight. The *Ben Vurie* sailed the next day with a steel patch welded over the corroded part of the plate and the bunks replaced.

The Fish Quay had its fair share of characters. Among these men was one called Danny the Gulp, who had obtained his name from his ability to drink a pint of beer without swallowing. As he drank his Adam's apple went up and down like a fiddlers elbow, hence his name. Danny had a large capacity for beer and was always drunk, that is when he had money to buy beer. This he obtained from working in the fish market in the early mornings, having spent the night before sleeping in the engine room of a trawler, which still had steam in the boiler. He never seemed to get washed and he stank to high heaven,

I once went onto a trawler and found him asleep on the boiler top, and he was just starting to smoulder. On being woken up he just grunted and shuffled away to get another drink in the Wooden Dolly pub. When I saw him a few days later he was still wearing his burnt clothes and was just as smelly. Every so often Danny would go into hospital to get sobered up, and when he came out you could hardly recognise him. He had put on weight, been given clean clothes, had his hair cut along with his beard, in fact he would be quite smart, but within a few hours he was back in the Dolly. Soon he was really drunk and back on a trawler to sleep it off, but you never heard of Danny hurting any one. He was just part of the fixtures and fittings on the Quay.

As with any occupation there are good jobs and bad jobs. Plumbers hated working on the fish room bilges but one incident will always remain sharp in my mind. It was mostly caused because the trawler was very old, and therefore comes under the general heading of the running of old ships, and the problems associated with them.

The trawler was SN 4 *Sarah Purdy* and when she docked at the Quay her skipper reported that the toilet was blocked. These toilets were very primitive, and consisted of a steel cubical attached to the crew's quarters up forward. Inside was a bowl to sit on but no running water to flush it, this water being obtained from over the side by means of a bucket. The plumbers did not want to clean this toilet unless they had to so they called on the services of a man called Mungo, who like Danny would do any thing for a hand out.

Mungo was rather different to Danny as he lived in a house somewhere and did not drink quite as heavily, but apart from these two things they were very similar in their approach to life. On being told what the job entailed, and accepting the amount offered, he started work. He borrowed the Haddock Shop's rowing boat, which allowed him to get at the discharge end of the toilet pipe. He then looked up the pipe and saw why it was blocked. Mungo tried to clear it with his 'bare hand', which was too big to go up the pipe, so he then climbed onto the deck of the trawler, and went looking for a long thin pole. After a time he returned with one, climbed back into the boat from the deck of the trawler and started to push the pole up the pipe. It only went a short way before it became firmly stuck in the blockage storm valve. It would not come out no matter how much he pulled and twisted that pole and in the end he went back on the deck and stood looking at the toilet, which by now was really blocked. The plumbers were getting quite worried as it looked as if they were going to get the job of clearing it.

A short while later Mungo was back to try again, but this time he poured water into the toilet before he climbed back into the boat and started to pull and twist. The water must have worked, as suddenly the pole came out along with what was in the toilet, plus the water. How long the blockage had been there we can only imagine and the whole lot went over Mungo covering him from head to toe. I shall not try to describe in any way what he looked or smelt like, I cannot, but as it was close to lunchtime he went home. An hour or so later Mungo returned. He looked no different to when he had left. Bits of unmentionable matter still clung to his clothes, his body and his hair. To make matters worse we were enjoying a nice hot summer day. We were about half way through our lunch hour and in the middle of our sandwiches. Mungo smelt like a swamp rat. We all ran out, it was just awful; in fact it was so bad that Alec also evacuated the Foreman's office next door. Mungo was completely unconcerned and settled down to eat his lunch, and most of ours as our appetites had for some reason disappeared.

After he had his solitary rest, out he came, and went back to the trawler and climbed back into the boat that was still half full with the contents of the toilet. Mungo proceeded to clean it out with his bare hands, stating that a little dirt never hurt anyone. Mungo got his money and for his part was quite happy.

I Thought I was A Hard Man until I joined the Trawler Ben Vurie

Les Campbell with his parents. Already he had aspirations of going to sea judging from his clothes.

The Fish Quay and the fishing boats are now a shadow of their former selves but the sight of a fishing boat returning to the quay still evokes many memories and is always of interest to bystanders. As the fishing boats sail steadily along the river safe inside the harbour bar, surrounded and followed by the incessant shrieking seagulls hoping for an easy meal, few people on shore have any idea what life is like a sea.

The grey hostile North Sea can change its mood quicker than a Fleet Street journalist. If anyone tells you that they are not frightened when they are at sea in a fishing boat at some time in their life then they are strangers to the truth.

Les Campbell was born in 1945 just before the end of the war. His father had lost a lung in the hostilities and like many others his grandmother brought up Les whilst the family sorted themselves out. Times were hard but Les never thought of himself as poor. He was like thousand of other kids in Wallsend. Les returned to the family home when they moved into council accommodation and it was then that he learned about the effects of alcohol. Both his parents were heavy drinkers and frequently imbibed in the 'liquid laughter' as Les calls it. Whether his observations of his parents were to set his pattern for later life Les does not know but he is the first to admit that he is an alcoholic despite the fact that he has not touched a drop for the past fifteen years.

Les in pensive mood with his mother.

Never an academic Les, like many others, saw his future in the shipyards and in 1961 he started his apprenticeship as a blacksmith at Swan Hunter's massive yard. An apprenticeship in a shipyard can be a daunting task but Les found it harder than most. By now, despite the fact that he was still only 16 years old he was a hardened drinker and a hangover and the din of a shipyard do not go together. Most days he seemed to have a hangover.

Les had only ten shillings a week pocket money after he had paid his board to his parents but this could not buy him the amount of drink that he wanted. He resorted to petty theft on a regular basis and three years into his apprenticeship he was dismissed from his employment for stealing copper and brass. Les could have walked away from the court with a fine or probation but he was out of control and rebellious. He acted the 'hard man' and the magistrates reciprocated. He was sentenced to six months at Medomsley Detention Centre for the short sharp shock treatment. It failed. His period in the Detention Centre acted as a college of knowledge and he was released with the mistaken belief that he was now really a 'hard man'. He now knew how to open safes, burgle premises, steal cars and brew illicit alcohol.

Crime now became his regular job but fortunately fate took a hand. An influential friend of his parents who worked at Swan Hunter's Shipyard saw salvation in Les and arranged for him to return to the yard to finish his apprenticeship. Somehow Les managed to pull it off and qualified as a blacksmith. Many a time in the docks he envied the sailors as they bustled about their ships, travelling to far off exotic places. He loved being on board a ship even if it was in dry dock and looked forward to the time when the dry dock was flooded and the ship floated again. He never lost the thrill of being on board whilst the ship was moved twenty or thirty yards to the jetty.

Drink and petty crime was still his stable daily diet although he managed to avoid being arrested. Work in the shipyards was fickle and depended upon orders. Inevitably the day came when the work dried up and Les was laid off. For many hundreds of men this was the accepted pattern of life. By now Les was married and lived with his wife Lillian in Gordon Square, Wallsend. These tenement flats were notorious for housing problem families and carried with them a social stigma if you lived there.

Time lay heavy without work and there was only so much money available to spend drinking. Les started walking from his home down to the North Shields Fish Quay. Why he did this he never really knew but something kept drawing him down to the Quay where he would sit for hours watching the trawlers and drifters docking or sailing for the fishing grounds. One day he was on the Quay when the *Ben Vurie* tied up at the Quayside. Les started a conversation with the crew and found out it was owned by Richard Irvin and Sons whose offices were just along from where the boat was berthed. Les walked into the offices and asked if there were any jobs going. The agent asked him if he had any sea experience and Les him told that he worked in the shipyards. The agent just roared with laughter but he could see that Les was keen and told him to come back the following day.

Les was true to his word and without mentioning anything to Lillian he returned to Richard Irvin's office. Les was taken up into the rigging loft where the nets were made and was given a crash course on mending nets. He passed with flying colours. He was given two weeks work on shore learning the rudiments of trawl fishing and he was told to return with a blanket. This he was later to find out was to be his bedding whilst at sea.

For two weeks he studiously learned all he could and then one day the agent announced that the *Ben Vurie* was sailing the next day and he was signed on for the trip. She was bound for the Faroes and Iceland. He was told to pick up some sea boots and waterproofs from the owners store and the cost of these would be deducted from his wages. Les was to be at sea for three weeks.

The *Ben Vurie* heading for the fishing grounds of Iceland and the Faroes.

That last night before he sailed was a strange affair. He told Lillian that he was sailing the next day and that she would have to survive on his 'dole money'. This was nothing knew for her but she seemed shell shocked whilst he was elated. He did not care as he was going to sea.

Early the next day armed with his blanket and waterproofs he boarded the *Ben Vurie* and met the skipper, 'Black Bob' Palmer. The skipper showed Les to his quarters, well really it was a cramped bunk along with another five bunks. The place reeked of cigarette smoke and Les did not smoke. The polluted air caught his breath. 'How can anyone feel comfortable in such a place' he thought. He was soon to find that he was never going to be in his bunk long enough to find how cramped it was.

Soon he assembled on deck with the rest of the crew and cast off. He was excited as they pulled away from the quay under the gaze of many onlookers. The trawler carried a bond of cigarettes and alcohol and Les was to find out his allowance was a dozen cans of beer and a bottle of whisky for the whole trip. This was hardly an aperitif for an alcoholic.

The *Ben Vurie* sailed out over the harbour bar in good weather and the crew settled down to two watches. This meant two hours on duty and two hours off duty.

Les' signing on papers showed that the trawler owner would pay him the sum of eight pounds per week depending on the size of the catch but the cost of the food he would consume, the cost of ice for the fish room and diesel oil together with any net repairs would come out of the profits of the catch before he was paid. Everything had a price.

Les joined the *Ben Vurie* at North Shields, having turned twenty years old, in the summer of 1967. He was the only rookie and he spent some time looking around and getting acquainted with the ship. The mate told him that he would be a fisherman by the time he was through with him.

Les was convinced that life as a fisherman held the promise of excitement and adventure. Anything had to be better than the shipyards. It did not take him long to become disillusioned. Backed up with knowledge of the arrogance of youth gained by his worldly experience of life and the fact that he still considered that he was a hard man he was sure he would be a natural seaman.

However once over the harbour bar and out into the open sea Les began to feel the deck move with the swell. It would be an exaggeration to say the ship was rolling, but it was enough to make him feel queasy. It was not long before he was violently sick all over the deck – 'I could not even make the side.'

He tried to take to his bunk, unable to cope with the nausea. When he had been at home he had always received every sympathy and he was sure it would be the same here. Everybody would be solicitous for his welfare. Wrong! It was not long before the mate appeared at his bunk. 'Les,' he demanded, 'you are due on watch.' He feebly acknowledged his responsibility. 'Get to it then!' he ordered.

To his seasick mind this was the height of callousness and it was only superseded when the skipper, came to him that evening. What consolation! 'The skipper cares,' he thought. He glanced at Les and said, 'Do you wish you were dead?' Les nodded weakly, at which point he chortled and left the cabin.

For three days until they reached the fishing grounds Les was violently sick. His blanket and bunk reeked of vomit as well as himself. Washing and shaving was forgotten about. He got used to his own smell and the others did not seem to mind. He neither slept nor ate for three days but he had to do his two-hour watches.

One of the crew came up with the ingenious idea of tying Les to the back of the funnel and told him to keep looking astern. Suddenly it worked. The seasickness abated, he was starving and the sickness was not to return. Les had gained his sea legs. Les was now a fisherman but he had learned a lesson. He was not really a hard man.

Les was amazed when they reached the Faroe Islands. The Faroes are notable for their remarkably changeable weather conditions, and the thunderstorms followed by thick fog. The eighteen inhabited islands of the Faroes group have a foreboding appearance. The wild beauty of the rugged islands, the sheer cliffs swarming with birds, the colossal stacks and tumbling waterfalls can probably best be appreciated from the sea. The unpolluted waters were rich in fish to which the Faroese have always looked, and from which they drew their prosperity. The *Ben Vurie* was there to prosper as well but at a price.

Force ten gales lashed at the boat but fishing went on. The seas seemed mountainous but Les had little time to think of this. They were catching fish, which is what they were there to do. They seemed to be constantly up to their waist in live fish and Les was amazed at the pressure they exerted as the squirmed and wriggled trying to get back into the sea. At times such as this a trawler becomes a floating slaughterhouse. The open deck is where the blood is spilt and the deckhands are the slaughter men. The work was hard and Les was sweating as he gutted the fish and threw them into the hold for packing in ice. All the time this was going on the trawler reared and bucked but the skipper was well experienced. He had been in these seas many times before. The crew rotated between being on deck and being down in the hold packing fish. Down in the hold was wet and cold due to the ice and the seawater that was being shipped aboard as the crew on top wrestled with the winches and the nets. However his own steaming sweat kept him comfortable if not pleasant to be standing beside. Stale sweat and fish make for a pungent combination.

Few people can imagine gutting fish on an open deck for eighteen hours at a time, gasping to breathe in the sharp air. Feeling the wind howling around your ears, being soaked to the skin by the showers of sea spray. Standing thigh deep in slimy fish on a cold wet deck, your fingers freezing cold and blue as the trawler pitches and rolls. Running for your life as a huge wave looms overhead. This is what Les experienced and the experience has lived with him all his life. He has no regrets and the trip ultimately made him a better person. And what is it all for? So someone could walk along a street with a greasy newspaper full of fish and chips.

During the trip one of the crew produced an urn containing a family members ashes. The skipper solemnly rang the ships bell and 'Bepe' scattered the ashes quickly over the foaming seas and probably some over himself. This greatly unnerved Les. For the next three nights he lay in his bunk wide eyed with fear. Strange noises had started coming from the ship's hull like a dull knocking. He was convinced that the dead person was trying to get back on board.

Day after day the routine of catching fish continued. This was no nine to five job. The trawler crew worked around the clock. Once fishing the day's work depends on the fish. If they are there, you worked. The weather on the whole of the trip seemed awful to Les but to an experienced fisherman this was his daily lot. Fish guts lay inches deep on the deck and had to be hosed off with a large hosepipe called a donkey. Not content with dealing with this offal the seagulls were always ready to take advantage of a quick and easy meal but they would gorge themselves to such an extent that they could not take off. Les, unlike many fishermen, tried to compassionate and would try to grab them to help them in the air. They responded by pecking him to bits.

Whilst the *Ben Vurie* and the crew battled with the elements and the difficulty of catching fish a political storm was brewing between Iceland and Great Britain. The Cod War was about to start. Time and again during the trip Icelandic Gunboats would charge towards the trawler and then change course at the last minute as they harried the *Ben Vurie*. If they thought that this would worry Skipper Bob Palmer they were wrong. He steadfastly continued fishing, treating their actions like those of a naughty child. Now Les realised what a 'hard man' was.

The view many fishermen dreaded whilst so far away from home. Fortunately on this occasion this warship is British.

Suddenly it was time to head for home. The three weeks had passed in a flash. Les had no idea what day it was but once the skipper announced they were turning for home the crew visibly cheered up. By now Les had been sober for almost three weeks, was black as the ace of spades and stank of fish. The smell of vomit had long been overtaken by the pervading smell of fish. If this was not bad enough, the store's rations had ran out so it was fish for breakfast, dinner and tea. Still it was fresh and the choice of fish was varied.

The run for home is time to sort out the nets and get the trawler cleaned up and ship shape as well as yourself. Soap and hot water start to appear and the air gets decidedly sweeter as the crew cleaned themselves, shaved and looked forward to getting ashore, even though for many it would be for only thirty-six hours and most of that time would have been spent in a public house. Talk revolves around which pub to go to and how big the fry was to be. The fry is a bag of fish, which all the crew are allowed for their own consumption. The fry was not supposed to be sold but many were. Les sold his for £5.

Les was not cured of his alcoholism due to this trip. As soon as he docked he went drinking in the Jungle, Uncle Tom's Cabin and the Ballarat. In this respect he was no different to the rest of the crew. They had all headed for the pubs where they would stay until they could no longer stand. They may have worked like horses to earn their money but once ashore they spent it like asses. Nevertheless, after three weeks risking their lives at sea, they deserved their fun ashore. Life between trips was at a high emotional level. They packed as much fun and drinking as they could into their short time ashore. Fights were inevitable but the pub brawl was just entertainment between themselves. All was forgotten the next day.

Somehow Les made it home and then it was off with Lillian to the Penny Wet pub in Wallsend. However time and tide wait for no one and soon it was time to return to the Arctic waters as the money was spent and the owners were anxious to get their boats back to sea. For Les there were to be no more trips. He never went back to sea as a trawler man. On his return his job at the shipyards as a blacksmith was back for him. The three-week trip however had a profound experience upon him. He realised that he could beat his problem with alcohol, he had missed being at home with Lillian and he had come to terms with the reality that he was no hard man. The true hard men were the fishermen he had just been to sea with.

Time has moved on for Les and Lillian. He is still a blacksmith and works and lives in Rosyth. He has not had a drink for fifteen years and is rehabilitated after serving a number of prison sentences. No longer a thief he is now a lay visitor at his local police station and he has become a pillar of his community. A belief in God and the ability to write poetry has replaced his desire for alcohol but he still considers himself an alcoholic. Les will never forget his three-week experience on the *Ben Vurie*. From a fisherman he is now a fisher of men.

TRAGEDY AND BRAVERY, A FISHERMAN'S LOT FOR THE ROSS FAMILY

Edward Teddy Ross is on the right. He was lost overboard whilst fishing off Iceland on 3rd December 1964.

Each individual's family is a fascinating pot pourri of experiences, tragedies, triviality, sadness and joy and anyone who has undertaken to research their family tree is aware of the difficulties that can be encountered.

The Ross family served North Shields well but like most of the families who made their living from the sea they had their share of tragedies. Tragedy and bravery make uneasy bedfellows but frequently went hand in hand throughout family life for many a family from North Shields.

James Ross was born in Limehouse, London in 1863 but it would seem that he was not called Ross. He was a foundling and had no surname. He became James Ross when he moved into North Shields and adopted this name. Why he chose the name Ross is open to speculation but by 1887 he had adopted this surname and since then all of the following family members on this side of the family have used the surname Ross, as this the only surname they have.

James Ross married Sarah Jane Smith on 1st January 1887 in North Shields. By this time he was a trawler man. Sarah Jane Smith was a native of North Shields and at the time of her marriage was five years younger than her husband. Their marriage produced ten children, all bar one of whom survived to adulthood.

William Octavius Ross was born in 1899 and by this time he had four brothers and a sister. Another brother had died within one month of being born. In 1919 he married Annie Murray who was two years older than him. They lived in Linskill Street, North Shields with their two sons and a daughter. In March 1932 he was a fisherman on board the North Shields boat, the *UgieBank*.

The *Ugiebank* was a Peterhead registered steam trawler, PD 85, and was typical of her breed. Built in 1913 at the height of the boom period in trawler fishing she was one of the many boats owned by Richard Irvin and Son of North Shields. The *Ugiebank* had a long and fairly uneventful life but unfortunately for William Ross he was not so lucky. Whilst at sea he was struck on the head and suffered a fractured skull. He survived long enough for him to be brought back to North Shields but died on 10th March 1932 in Tynemouth Infirmary. Had he survived into old age I am sure he would have been proud of his younger brother John Clements Ross.

The armed trawler is not an ideal anti-submarine craft but the trawler proved that they could be exceedingly effective against their larger enemy. Too small to be worth a torpedo, the Patrol Service trawler with its scanty weapons, lack of armour and slow speed stood very little chance in a straight fight against the guns of a surfaced U-boat. The same considerations rendered the average minesweeping or anti-submarine trawler little more than a sitting duck for the swooping dive-bombers of the Luftwaffe; swift and powerfully armed E-boats could brush these lumbering escorts contemptuously aside in their darting attacks on our coastal convoys; larger hostile surface units could blast the average Patrol Service craft out of existence like a giant swatting a fly. Nevertheless time was to show that the enemy was by no means going to have things all his own way with the little ships. Sublimely indifferent to the hazards they were about to face, the men of the Navy's Lilliputian Fleet sallied forth to do battle.

Brave to the end – A tribute to all who lost their lives

Christmas Day 1942, off the east coast of Scotland the North Shields trawler SN 78 *Ben Screel* was lashed by rain and pitching drunkenly on a rising sea hove anchor. She was going to fish. About her, huddled, as though for protection against the squall were other little vessels of the fleet. Watchful eyes saw the drab of the *Ben Screel* merge into the grey dawn. She was never seen again.

It dawned on North Shields eventually that David Tawse McRuvie MBE and the nine gallant fishermen who formed her crew had shot their last trawl. For some time afterwards, although the crew no longer came in and out of the port they were still talked about, for they were fighters as well as fishermen. Skipper McRuvie, a native of Fifeshire, and his crew had combed the sea for fish whilst watching the sky for German raiders but their fight had been lost.

Before the *Ben Screel* was lost she had been involved in action with the enemy whilst trying to go about her mercantile duties. On 2nd June 1941 out of the clouds had swooped two German planes and the weather beaten fingers of William Charles Jarman, of Whitstable, deck hand and gunner tightened on his Lewis Gun. An aerial torpedo came straight at him. It missed Jarman and the flimsy wooden shield around him, tore through a skylight, travelled along the engine room and galley, narrowly missing two men warming themselves at the galley stove and left the ship through the bulwarks exploding as it hit the water. Off came the rudder of the *Ben Screel*.

Then another plane came in. Jarman had been blown from his post and was dazed by the explosion but he got to his gun and greeted the incoming German aircraft with a stream of bullets. Some found their mark and the aircraft veered off severely damaged. Jarman did not expect the enemy aircraft to make it back to land. His job was done.

The *Ben Screel* was now badly damaged and rudderless. A jury rudder was fitted using one of the trawl boards and the *Ben Screel* limped safely back to port, a distance of one hundred miles. For their part in this action Skipper McRuvie received the MBE and Jarman's heroism was rewarded by the BEM.

Five months later, on 12th November 1941, the *Ben Screel* was back in the fishing grounds when they were again attacked by an enemy aircraft that launched a bomb at them. The bomb skidded across the concrete covered wheelhouse and buried itself in the rigging without exploding.

Then came 9th December 1942 when the Ben Screel sailed for the last time from North Shields. Skipper McRuvie and Jarman were still in the crew. On the 17th of December 1942 they put into Methil for one night and then off back out into the grey, hostile North Sea.

Admiralty records state that the vessel was lost off St Abbs Head on Christmas Day 1942 with a loss of all life.

The guns that were mounted were of a smaller calibre than those carried by U-boats but on the other hand a U-boat is far more vulnerable to damage by gunfire than any surface craft. A submarine cannot afford to risk her hull being holed for that, even if it did not prove fatal, would make it impossible for her to dive and would thus deprive her of her only defence against any more powerful men-of-war that she might encounter. It is therefore possible for even a trawler, engaging a U-boat to force her to dive by good shooting. Once under water the U-boat is slow and, moreover, becomes liable to attack by depth charges, which the trawler can carry just as well as larger or faster men-of-war. Thus the trawler can provide with her 12-pounder forward gun and a load of depth charges aft a mean antagonist for the U-boat. What at first sight might appear to a 'David versus Goliath' battle was quickly to be equalised by the dogmatism of the crew and the manoeuvrability of the armed trawler.

HMT *Fyldea* in the English Channel. Typical of her breed, these tiny boats performed sterling service against the deadly submarine.

Minesweeping of course comes almost naturally to the fishermen who man the trawlers. The task of handling and towing the minesweepers is almost the same thing as their ordinary occupation of handling the trawl.

From the outset it was evident that the pattern of the sea war would be repeated by the enemy even more ruthlessly than in 1914-18. On the evening of the 3rd September 1939, the 13,581 ton Donaldson liner *Athenia*, with 1,418 passengers and crew, was torpedoed without warning and sunk some 250 miles west of Ireland. On the same day U-boats laid mines off the Tyne, Humber and in the Thames Estuary.

At the outbreak of war, trawler production was gradually increased to meet the need for suitable anti-submarine and minesweeping vessels. An increasing amount of mercantile trawlers were also requisitioned and fitted out for war. These included Arctic whalers and the wooden constructed drifters first used during the First World War.

The tough and enduring sea worthiness of the trawler was seen to be an ideal choice for an escort vessel. This enabled the vessel to deployed in the roughest of seas, which would often even force a larger ship, such as a destroyer, to seek shelter.

Naval trawlers were produced mostly during the course of the Second World War as number of small shipyards specialised in this type of ship and their resources were ideally suited to the Admiralty. The order was given for the construction of new trawlers based on the commercial designs that could be readily modified into escorts and minesweepers.

Generally to transform a trawler into a man-of-war, a considerable amount of modification had to be carried out. To carry the guns, hull frames and deck beams had to be strengthened. At the front of the ship on the forecastle, and situated on the whaleback, a 12-pounder or four-inch was mounted. Aft (or rear) of the funnel, a purpose built mounting was fitted to hold an Oerlikon, Bofors or a pair of five-inch machine guns. For the added protection against air attack, Lewis or Hotchkiss guns were fitted in the bridge wings. For vessels destined for anti-submarine work depth-charge throwers and rails would also be fitted along with the necessary Asdic equipment for detecting enemy submarines.

Alterations to a trawler's basic design were also carried out in order to accommodate a larger crew, usually around 30 or so for the average anti-submarine trawler, including at least two skippers. The fish-hold became the main ship's company mess deck with wooden mess tables and stools. Above in this confined and cramped area, hung hammocks from the beams in any available space. Sometimes the Stokers (often nicknamed the black gang) had a separate mess. Usually below the mess deck and in a specially constructed magazine, was stored the ammunition for the ship's guns. The officers' quarters were situated below the wheelhouse and contained a couple of bunks along with some basic furniture, a cupboard and a safe for confidential books. Lastly a small galley was included, where one cook had the impossible task of keeping an entire crew happy with the sparsest of wartime provisions.

At sea these cramped conditions were anything but ideal and in a heavy storm they could soon become very uncomfortable. This was particularly hard on those men who had not been part of the peacetime fishing fleet and therefore had no previous experience of life at sea. A small ship such as a trawler will always ride the waves rather than push a path through them like a larger vessel. As a result the pitch and roll of a small ship in a heavy swell will make the simplest of tasks almost impossible.

The *Scire* was one of Italy's premier submarines and was launched in 1938. She was an 850-ton vessel, 197 feet in length, and had a surface speed of fourteen knots. Her original armament had included a 3.9 inch gun mounted forward of the conning tower but soon after Italy's entry into the war the *Scire's* big gun had been removed and three long steel cylinders fitted to her casing instead, one forward of the conning-tower and two aft. The *Scire*, operating patrols along the Mediterranean from Gibraltar to Egypt, specialised in the use of 'maiali' human torpedoes. These torpedoes, manned by Italian junior naval officer volunteers, achieved notable successes against British shipping. These were not, as often erroneously reported, suicide weapons. They were steered by the operator until close to the target, the operator then locking the steering and sliding into the water. In the successful 'maiali' action at the end of 1941 the *Scire* sank the battleships *Queen Elizabeth* and *Valiant*, the destroyer *Jervis* and the tanker *Sagona* in the shallow waters off the port of Alexandria.

HMS *Queen Elizabeth* sunk in the shallow waters off Alexandria, Egypt by the 'human torpedoes' from the Scire during the night 18/19th December 1941. She was salvaged but was out of action for twelve months.

The Lilliputian fleet was scattered far and wide and one action almost a year later brought a welcome ray of light to the gloomy situation in the eastern Mediterranean. With the Eighth Army forced back to the Alamein Line by Rommel's army the threat to Alexandria compelled a hurried dispersal of the British warships based in that port. Some retired to the Red Sea, others to Haifa. Aware of the dispersal of British warships caused by the Axis threat to Egypt, the Italians planned an attack on those that had been moved to Haifa, to be carried out by frogmen using limpet charges. *Scire's* hull was painted pale green and to camouflage her she had daubed along her sides, ironically enough, the silhouette of a trawler. In command was an experienced submariner Lieutenant-Commander Bruno Zclich.

Patrolling off the swept channel of Haifa was the anti-submarine trawler *Islay* under the command of Skipper Lieutenant John Clements Ross, RNR, the eighth child of the union between James Ross and Sarah Jane Smith. John Clements Ross was born in 1900 and had married Ada Emma Kenny in 1921. Within seven years of the marriage they were the proud parents of three sons and a daughter.

The *Islay* was an Admiralty designed vessel, one of the 'Isles' class, or which more than hundred and forty-five were built for the Patrol Service during the war. The *Islay* was the only one of the Isles class to be built by Smith's Dock of North Shields and Middlesbrough and it is fitting that a local man commanded her.

Among the first dozen to be launched in the spring of 1941, the *Islay* displaced 545 tons, was 164 feet long with a 27-foot beam. She carried a complement of thirty-three officers and men, could steam at fifteen knots and was able to range over three thousand miles of ocean without refuelling. In build she was more compact than the average fishing trawler of comparable tonnage, with a larger bridge and an additional gun sponson on the forward well deck. The 'Isles' class were designed to mount a four-inch gun on the forecastle as their main armament but, at the time the *Islay* distinguished herself against the Italian Navy, she carried only a 12-pounder forward and twin point-fives guns aft.

On 10th August 1942, the *Scire* stealthily approached Haifa. Four days previously, the *Scire* had quietly slipped her moorings off the island of Leros intent on reeking havoc on the British warships anchored in Haifa harbour.

At about two o'clock in the afternoon the Asdic operator on board the *Islay* reported a submarine contact. At once Ross went into action, and a few minutes later his first pattern of depth charges were on their way. However the trawler captain ran out too far on his attack and contact was lost. Patiently he commenced a search and shortly afterwards, to his relief, the empty pinging of the Asdic was replaced by unmistakable submarine echoes. It was clear from their nature that the vessel was now lying stopped. Ross, believing that his first pattern had damaged the U-boat, sent another six-charge pattern arcing astern and into the shallow seas to add to her troubles.

Opening the range to four hundred yards while the depth charges were convulsing the ocean in his wake Ross swung his vessel round in time to witness a heartening sight. The *Scire* porpoised to the surface spouting water from the vents of her ballast tanks as her pale green hull showed itself. Almost immediately the camouflage-daubed hull began to founder by the stem. The *Islay's* point five guns opened up their ear-splitting racket to be followed almost immediately by the sharp bark of her 12-pounder. The gunners on board the *Islay* were up to their task. For just as long as it took the trawler gunners to load and fire seventeen rounds from the 12-pounder the submarine continued its crazy floundering after she took hit after hit. In all Ross counted twelve direct hits.

The *Scire* was finished and went into her death throws. Quickly she began to slip back, seeming to hang suspended by her vertically pointed nose like a dying shark before she finally plunged beneath the surface to the seabed below.

The *Scire* was mortally wounded but in war the total destruction of the enemy must be ensured. The *Islay* steamed over to the spot where the concentric wavelets were still spreading to administer the final coup de grâce. Six more depth charges spun into the air and sank into the pale depths. Once again the sea heaved in violent tumult and as the trawler finally turned and headed for harbour a vast oil patch covered the area. From its centre bubbles slowly rose, each as it burst releasing a tiny cloud of fetid green gas. Fifty-nine Italian sailors perished in the *Scire*.

Four days later the bodies of two Italian sailors were washed ashore in Haifa, and were buried with full naval honours. In Rome a gold medal for gallantly was pinned to the flag of the submarine *Scire*, a crack unit of the Fascist underwater fighters, whose nemesis had been a little British trawler. Commander Ross received the Distinguished Service Cross for his bravery and command during the sinking of the *Scire*.

Edward Locke Ross, who was known by everyone as 'Teddy', was the last child born to James and Sarah Ross. Like his father and two brothers the sea quickly beckoned and he became a trawler man. Teddy was a popular trawler man on the Fish Quay in the early sixties. By now the fishing industry was on the wane and the newer oil fired boats had replaced nearly all of the steam trawlers. Conditions on board these vessels were much improved over the aged coal burners but the sea was no less of a dangerous place.

Teddy Ross, aged 51 years, was a deck hand on board the North Shields registered SN 85 *Ben Strome*. Built in 1962 she was a fine looking modern vessel and like the *Ugiebank* was owned by Richard Irvin and Son. This was not the first time that an Irvin boat had carried this name. The original *Ben Strome*, registered as A 109, was built in 1914. In 1941 she was sunk by a German aircraft off the Faroe Islands but fortunately without any loss of life.

SN 85 *Ben Strome*.

On 3rd December 1964 the *Ben Strome* was fishing in the bitingly cold seas off Iceland. The heavy swell was making things difficult and the weather conditions freezing. Bob Casson was working alongside Teddy as they hauled in the nets with what appeared to be a reasonable catch. Suddenly the ship and the crew were swamped by two heavy waves that carried the fish back into the sea. Three crewmembers including Alfred Brown, 35 years of Dockwray Square, North Shields and Teddy Ross were thrown onto the deck by the force of the water. Teddy was seen to be floating in the water and managed to grab a handrail and pull himself onto the winch platform amidships. The skipper called all the men back into the safety of the boat and came down with a bottle of rum to ease life back into their frozen limbs. They were soaking wet and cold. As they changed their clothing someone asked where Teddy was. No one knew. They assumed he had gone below to fetch dry clothing. A quick search revealed that Teddy was nowhere to be found. Teddy Ross had been carried overboard and was lost at sea. Life expectancy in such conditions was measured in single minutes but nevertheless they searched for Teddy and informed nearby boats of their loss. The body of Teddy Ross was never recovered.

The inquiry later held into his unfortunate death of Teddy Ross concluded, 'It remains a mystery and is one of the hazards of a fisherman's life.'

Acknowledgements

I am indebted to the many people who contacted me after my first book *Beyond the Piers* went on sale and also to those people, who without solicitation left me photographs, memories, and stories with Martin Pontin at William Wight's on the Fish Quay.

I am constantly amazed at the generosity of people, many of whom I have sometimes never met, in allowing me to use stories which are personal and sometimes do not portray them in a good light at some time during their life. These stories enrich my books and show that there is good in most people.

LT 46 *Silver Crest* prepares to depart from North Shields Fish Quay.

My books are written from the heart but I have an admission to make. I have never been to sea on a trawler or a drifter. I would have liked to but the opportunity has never arisen. Perhaps the experience would have negated my passion for recording people's experiences, as I would have become blasé about the danger, the difficulties, and the sheer hard work that fishermen accept as their daily lot in life.

I would like to specifically thank the following people:
Les Campbell, Mike Ennis, Kenneth Banks, Martin Pontin (again), Bob Casson, Brian Reeds, Joseph Ackley, Bill Davidson, Bob Dixon, Thomas Bailey, Jimmy Cullen (again), Alfie Walker, Peter Burns and the facilities on offer at North Shields Library. I must also especially thank Danny Nicholson of Nicholsons Prints for allowing me to use many of his modern day Fish Quay photographs.

The Author

The author, Ron Wright is a retired Detective Chief Inspector who served in Northumberland County Constabulary, Northumberland Constabulary and Northumbria Police. He lives in Cullercoats with his wife Margaret and their dogs. He has two grown up children, a son Christopher and a daughter Jacqueline who live in the area.

Although a native of Newcastle he has had an affinity with North Shields, in particular the Fish Quay since his teenage years and his wife Margaret was born overlooking the Fish Quay.

This is Ron's third book within the last twelve months. His first book *Beyond the Piers – A Tribute to the Fishermen of North Shields* created so much interest that this second book on the Fish Quay area had to be written.

His other book *Cullercoats – A Unique Village, a Special Place to Live* chronicles the history of the village and gives a special insight to a way of life, which has now disappeared.

Ron could not have achieved his task so thoroughly had it not been for the unselfish assistance of the people whom he acknowledges in all his books. Their generosity seems to have no bounds.

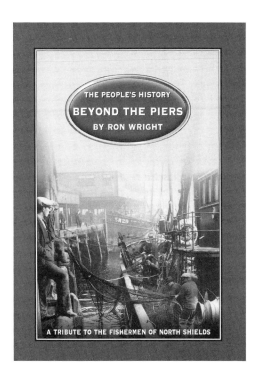

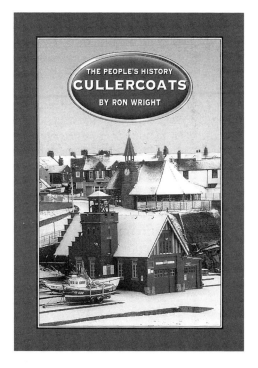

A dramatic illustration of how dangerous life can be for a fisherman. The Grimsby trawler GY 489 *Hassett* lies wrecked and lost to the sea off Caithness, Scotland in 1953.

The People's History

To receive a catalogue of our latest titles send a large SAE to:

The People's History
Suite 1
Byron House
Seaham Grange Business Park
Seaham
County Durham
SR7 0PY